Belgium, Come Forth!

Healing (from) the Heart of Europe

Armour

DEBORAH DEKKER

Foreword — Anne Hamilton

Introduction — Anne Griffith

Appendix — Jean-Antoine

Afterword — Ignace Demaerel

Belgium, Come Forth! Healing (from) the Heart of Europe

© Text: Deborah Dekker 2021

Published by Armour Books
P. O. Box 492, Corinda QLD 4075 AUSTRALIA

Cover Image: This painting is a variation of the flag of Belgium, based on the prophetic word given about this flag and mentioned in chapter 10. It has been made by artist Paul Verheul (https://paulverheul.com), at the request of the author.

Page 11 Photograph: Jon Tyson/Unsplash

Interior Design and Typeset by Beckon Creative

ISBN: 9781925380354

A catalogue record for this book is available from the National Library of Australia

Please note: this book uses Australian spelling and grammar conventions.

And as for your birth, on the day you were born your cord was not cut, nor were you washed with water to cleanse you, nor rubbed with salt, nor wrapped in swaddling cloths. No eye pitied you, to do any of these things to you out of compassion for you, but you were cast out on the open field, for you were abhorred, on the day that you were born. "And when I passed by you and saw you wallowing in your blood, I said to you in your blood, 'Live!' I said to you in your blood, 'Live!'

Ezekiel 16:4–7 ESV

The hand of the Lord was upon me, and He brought me out in the Spirit of the Lord and set me down in the middle of the valley; it was full of bones. And He led me around among them, and behold, there were very many on the surface of the valley, and behold, they were very dry. And He said to me, "Son of man, can these bones live?" And I answered, "O Lord God, You know." Then He said to me, "Prophesy over these bones, and say to them, O dry bones, hear the word of the Lord. Thus says the Lord God to these bones: Behold, I will cause breath to enter you, and you shall live. And I will lay sinews upon you, and will cause flesh to come upon you, and cover you with skin, and put breath in you, and you shall live, and you shall know that I am the Lord."

Ezekiel 37:1–6 ESV

Endorsements

Deborah is for many years a faithful intercessor in and for Belgium, and has a warm heart for this nation. Loving your nation also means suffering for her, feeling her pain. During the years she has gathered many precious prophetic insights. Every time we worked or prayed together, it was a joy to do so, in bridging the gap between the north and south of the country. May this book also call forth God's passionate cry for your nation, which only He can pour out in your heart.

Ignace Demaerel
Pastor, Author
Leader of *Pray for Belgium*
www.pray4belgium.be

Great book—absolutely love it!

Before your very eyes, the story of our nation is displayed.

Deborah writes here with the hope in mind for all to see and know that prayer is paramount for a nation to rise up. She displays everything so well and clearly both in the natural and spiritual world. After reading this book, you can do nothing but intercede, not only for Belgium, but also for the 27 European nations that gather on Belgian territory.

Be inspired by this book and speak to Belgium: Come forth!

Luc and Agnès Depreter
Pastors of *Heartbeat Church*
Organisers of the *One in Christ Conferences*, Belgium

We are very excited about this latest book by Deborah, "Belgium, Come Forth!"

I believe it is a book written in season to release a word over this nation in sync with what the Spirit of God is doing and releasing in this nation. It is more than an informational book but rather a prophetic decree which will equip readers to understand what is happening spiritually, as well as to pray and intercede accordingly. It gives us strategic weapons of warfare to intercept the specific plans of the enemy by exposing them and releasing God's truth and purposes and promises over this country! It is truly a book written for a "time such as this"!

We not only recommend the book but also the author. Deborah is a gifted writer who humbly carries the gift of prophecy and discernment. She has a tremendous heart for Belgium and to see God's kingdom released over this land! We are grateful for her obedience in releasing what the Lord has given her and we highly encourage leaders, pastors, intercessors working in Belgium and Europe to give this a read!

Natalia and Ricky Venter
Lead Pastors
Vineyard Brussels

Deborah has been a dear friend for many years. Together we have prayed many times for our country, Belgium. She has always been a model of fervour and love for this land which, in its history, has been so abused.

In this book, Deborah opens, with the Holy Spirit, the scrolls of the land of Belgium. She sends forth a prophetic cry that calls for repentance, healing and restoration.

Deborah drew on her unparalleled and well-documented knowledge of the history of our land, as well as revelations from the Spirit of Prophecy, so it's no wonder these writings contain some real treasures.

Thank you, Deborah, for daring to embrace your mission by writing this book, which was in dire need of being brought into the world. Thank you for your sensitivity to the voice of the Lord, as well as for your obedience and tenacity.

May this book open the eyes of many to the reality of the battlefield on which we find ourselves and give them the right leads in order to intercede for our land of Belgium.

Jean-Antoine
French-speaking Author
Belgium

I have known Deborah for many years now. As long as I remember, she has always been passionate about our country, our Belgium, which is more than "the poor little Belgium", as some see in it.

More than loving Belgium, Deborah has it in her womb.

Reading her book is captivating: she has listened to the Spirit and let her prophetic pen speak to tell us what the Lord says over Belgium today.

And though it is not, as she says, a book of history, Deborah's knowledge of Belgium's story, put together with her sensitivity to the Spirit, opens your eyes and your heart to another side of its history.

If you read it, allowing the Spirit to speak through the written words, you can feel the Lord's desire for Belgium to be restored and His call for the country to fulfill its mandate, according to what has been written in its book in heaven.

You can feel something new stirring in your spirit: a new dimension of intercession, aligned to the Spirit's voice.

*Thank you, Deborah, for daring write this book, in obedience to the Lord.
It is precious for all those who have nations in their hearts.*

Sabrina Mahieu
Prophetic School Rehoboth
Belgium (Wallonia)

*Deborah's book is a treasure trove full of hidden insights into the
spiritual background of beautiful Belgium. An invaluable tool for all
with a heart for the healing of this land and its people.*

Moyra Sims
Ellel Ministries
Belgium

*It would seem this book has come for such a time as this as we see many
things happening in the nation of Belgium. I have been twice to Belgium
and only wish I could have read this excellent book before my trips. I
would have been better equipped to minister with the history of this
amazing and important nation. Hope it gives you as it did me a new love
for BELGIUM and a renewed desire to pray for her.*

Barbara Smith
Prophetic Ministry
Scotland

TABLE OF CONTENTS

Foreword

Anne Hamilton

'For such a time as this...'

The world that we live in is ordered by the steady drumbeat of *chronos* time. The clocks on our walls relentlessly count down the hours. Calendars impose a rigorous schedule across our days and years, with only an occasional 'moveable feast' to vary the strict regimen. Our lives are fenced by boundary-marker dates—commemorations and celebrations.

Yet Scripture testifies to different ways of understanding time.

A century ago, in the Weimar Republic of the 1920s, the Kairos Circle was inspired by Paul Tillich's biblically derived notion of *kairos* time—a fulfilled time. Tillich's thought is described by Daniel Weidner as a divine irruption where "every moment might be the small gate through which the messiah will enter."

15

Kairos was conceived of as a radical incursion by God into history, to upend and overturn hypocritical façades of church and state. Yet, in the coming of Jesus to our world, He never tore up the tapestry of history, He always mended it. Sometimes quietly and unobtrusively, sometimes with a fanfare and a flourish.

Always perfectly.

He went to a town where, a thousand years in the past, the kingship had been lost to the royal line, ripped away in a fractious rebellion against slavery. That same town was a place where five leaders and patriarchs had reaffirmed their covenant with the God of Israel. And one had broken it.

It was a town in the same territory where, hundreds of years previously, women had gone after being shamed, divorced and expelled from Jerusalem at the command of a priest and a cupbearer.

It was a town where the original inhabitants had covenanted with the tribes of Israel, yet were slaughtered in revenge for a rape.

Who could represent such a complex, wounded land? Could there be a person with six covenantal relationships, five good, one bad? Could that someone also have the power to restore the kingship back to the line of David? Could that someone furthermore understand the pain of shame, divorce and expulsion? Would that someone, despite everything, consider an appointment as cupbearer and ambassador for the King of Kings?

Now Jesus, said John, *"had to go through Samaria."* (John 4:4 NIV) Interesting, isn't it, that phrase *"had to go"*? Because there were ways to avoid Samaria. But there was a *kairos* moment, an appointed time to be fulfilled, needing His attention.

A five-times-married woman was about to head for an ancient well at Sychar near the town of Shechem and, for her, "the small gate through which the messiah will enter" was about to swing open. Everything would hinge on how she responded to His initial invitation to be His cupbearer: *"Will you give Me a drink?"* (John 4:7 NIV)

It seems almost too ordinary, doesn't it? That this simple question should be the first stitch in a mending of the history of a torn and traumatised town.

This healing combination of land and people was not a unique event in the life of Jesus. Healing history was a major component of His ministry: He did it when He went to Jericho, to Emmaus, when He sent out seventy disciples to the villages of Galilee and Samaria, when He walked from Bethany-beyond-the-Jordan to Bethany outside of Jerusalem.

He healed history before He died and He accelerated His efforts after He was resurrected.

And each time He set about 'mending the world', He did it differently. He had no formula. His actions were tailored to the individual history of each special location. It's all too easy to miss what He did because we dismiss the geographical clues given to us by the gospel writers and we don't bother to look up the history of the place they've mentioned.

The earth is waiting for redemption. Like the rest of creation, it longs to be released from futility and trauma and it strains *"on tiptoe to see the wonderful sight of the sons of God coming into their own."* (Romans 8:19 JB Phillips)

Just as Jesus had to go through Samaria, He has to go through Belgium. His plan for its healing is matchless, inimitable, unique. But that He does have a plan, I have no doubt. It comes at His appointed time, His *kairos* moment. We have to be prepared for it because it may come when we least expect it.

For several years now, I've been writing about *Jesus and the Healing of History*. I saw how Jesus did it—sometimes secretly and sometimes spectacularly—and I longed to be present at such a moment but hardly dared hope for it. Because one thing I have learned: the exactly right representatives are as necessary as the exactly right time. Yet very recently I was thrilled when I witnessed such a *kairos* hour. My heart leapt with such great delight, I thought of the words of Mrs Beaver in *The Chronicles of Narnia* when she meets the four children for the first time: "So you've come at last! … At last! To think that ever I should live to see this day!"

For Belgium, as for other nations, the time is near when we will arise and say: "So you've come at last! … At last! To think that ever I should live to see this day!"

Be ready, be expectant! He's coming!

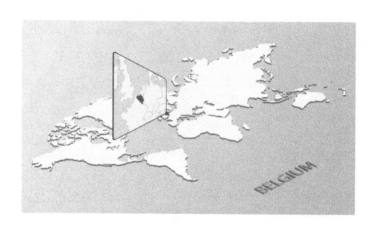

Preface

Deborah Dekker

The call to write about my homeland, Belgium, is not a recent one.

Somehow, it all began long ago, with the meeting in Brussels of my father and my mother and the merging of two cultures, languages and family lineages (my father being Dutch-speaking with a family coming from the Netherlands, my mother French-speaking coming from Wallonia—each with a deep respect and love for the language of the other).

Then, in 2018, when I was drafting my first book on *Fathers*,[1] this is what I wrote as an introduction:

> *I am writing this from a special country. A country which to a certain extent is itself an orphan, as it was created as a buffer zone in Europe following the defeat of Napoleon at Waterloo.*

---

1 Deborah Dekker, *Fathers: The Heart of the Father—The Cry of the Sons*, Armour Books, July 2019.

The British and the Austrians presided at its birth with the Dutch and Germans leaning upon the cradle. France ceded a small part of its territory to allow it to come into existence; as did the Netherlands too. The mother tongue of its inhabitants has always been problematic along with its national identity. Belgium, for this is the country in question, is also the country of (the two murdered girls) Julie and Melissa, of the 'white marches'[2] ... a country where certain deep wounds are difficult to heal, where healing balm seems to be missing. Where the voices which could cry out to make complaints and demand justice seem to be lacking—or at least fail to make enough noise.

Where the question of the validity of presenting one's case whether before a human or heavenly judgment seat can fail at the crucial moment.

Where the Church, called to defend the widow and the orphan (as well as the mourning parent) often itself seems dumb or paralyzed...

Somehow, Belgium was present in my heart and writing from the beginning.

Yet the thought of dedicating a whole book to this very special country emerged at the same time as the second book

---

2 This refers to the Dutroux case, the kidnapping, child abuse and murder of young girls in Belgium. A number of shortcomings in the Dutroux investigation caused widespread discontent in Belgium with the country's criminal justice system. In the White March of October 1996, 300,000 Belgian citizens protested the mishandling of the case.

on *Mothers* [3] appeared before my eyes. From that moment on, I knew there would be a triplet of books, *Fathers, Mothers,* and somehow, because of the peculiar birthing of the vision, which I called at that time *"Baby Belgium"* or, rather, the birth (or rebirth) of Belgium.

Then the National Day of Prayer for Belgium came along (2020 on Zoom because of COVID-19), with its theme, *"For such a time as this"*, and I was asked [4] if I would be willing to lead a time of intercession for Belgium, on a topic of my choice.

While praying about what this topic should be, I got the sense that we would have to pray about "the birth wound" or "birth trauma" of Belgium. I submitted this impression to the leadership team organising the event and it was approved after prayer. So began the preparations. I had invited a few French-speaking brothers and sisters to join me for this session. One of them was my friend Jean-Antoine, who is a psychologist and Christian writer. I asked him to expand on what a birth trauma is and what the consequences could be of having experienced this, in the life of a person—or a country.

Many people were touched that day. They also gave us feedback that they were not very familiar with the history of

---

3 Deborah Dekker, *Mothers: Battle for Birth*, published by Armour Books, September 2020, in a combined version with Fathers.

4 By Ignace Demaerel, dear Flemish brother and leader of the movement *Pray for Belgium*. He has been organising national days of prayer for Belgium for more than 10 years. See www.pray4belgium.be for more details.

Belgium nor with the aspects which had been presented that day. They said such insight and revelatory knowledge should be put down on paper.

It took me a while to come to terms with the content of the book, especially in the context of COVID-19 which has, in many ways, rearranged the gathering of prayer groups in the country as well as the vision some prophetic voices began to have about Belgium.

Another question, not so easy to handle, was that of the language for this book about Belgium. Having French as my mother tongue, yet with a deep respect for each language group in our nation, either French or Dutch seemed the natural choice.

But the idea was also to make the spiritual history of Belgium available to international intercessors who had revealed a lack of information on the subject as well as their desire to pray and intercede for what could still be unhealed wounds in the land.

The British Empire was very much involved in the birthing process of Belgium around the battle of Waterloo, as were other nations. A book written in French or Dutch could not so easily be read by intercessors in these other countries. So, after much prayer and reflection, the language chosen for the writing of this book was English.

As for the structure of this book, it follows the same outline as the first two volumes on *Fathers and Mothers*. The vision of "triplet books", each very much linked one with the other, is reflected in the three-part structure of THE CRY – THE CHALLENGE – THE ANSWER, each section divided into chapters.

This is not a history book. As many excellent books concerning different chapters of the factual history of Belgium have already been written (some mentioned in the notes), my intention is not to try to add to, or compete with, these. Rather this is a book about the spiritual inheritance and destiny of Belgium—a book that could function as a guide for prophetic intercession in order to further heal the heart of Europe.[5]

Yet it is not a mere manual, with bullet points for prayer: emotions are shared and poems written by artists are reproduced, so you can "feel" the spiritual atmosphere and challenge of the land, and have your heart of compassion stirred on behalf of Belgium.[6]

In order to do that, some elements of information, some historic facts, have to be briefly shared, which happens mostly in the second part of the book: *The Challenge*. These are briefly summarised, as my intention is to stress the spiritual aspects and consequences of those facts. References are made to material broadly available, but often not sufficiently known; sources are quoted.

---

5 To say it in other words: often the ones who pray do not know the historical facts, and the ones who know the facts often do not pray. This book tries to bridge that gap.

6 For an excellent manual with prayer points, you can read the booklet written by Ignace Demaerel, *Spiritual Climate of Belgium*, with 30 prayer topics, www.pray4belgium.be/en/english/resources.

The last part, *The Answer*, turns from past into future and destiny, with a strong invitation, for such a time as this: *Belgium, Come Forth!*

The introduction by Anne Griffith, prophet to the nations, lover of and visitor to Belgium for many years, and the chapter on birth trauma by Jean-Antoine, psychologist and prophetic writer from Wallonia, are not "addenda" but essential parts of this book. They also broaden the spiritual perspective that it is possible to have for a country as diverse, multilingual and multi-faceted as Belgium.

May your emotions be touched since, when you are "touched with compassion", real intercessory prayer can happen—and, sometimes, even resurrection![7]

May the breath of the Spirit blow on you and on the following pages, may the love of the Father kindle your hearts as you read about "brave little Belgium"... or, as other precious brothers and sisters love to say, "beautiful Belgium"!

---

7 See the chapter on Lazarus' resurrection in John 11 and the intense emotions depicted there: *Jesus wept...Then the Jews said, "See how He loved him!"... Jesus, once more deeply moved, came to the tomb... "Take away the stone," He said... Jesus called in a loud voice, "Lazarus, come out!" The dead man came out...*

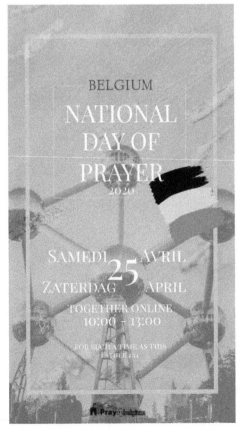

Introduction

Anne Griffith

For the Love of Belgium

Have you ever so deeply loved a nation that you wanted to hold her and love her back to life? Some nations do that to your heart. You cannot love like that unless it is given to you by the Lord. If He can do that to our heart, can we ever imagine what the divine heart of God feels at the brokenness He sees?

Some nations are easy to love, others can frustrate all attempts to "make them better". We do like to make things better sadly, whatever your "better" might be. Christians, non-believers. We all have our ideas for improvement. Nations can make you sad, mad or downright cynical—all at the same time. It is all part of the process and the pain cannot be avoided if you want to truly share in God's heart for any one of the nations alive right now on planet Earth.

From glory to dust—God's ways with the nations

> *He (God) makes nations great, then destroys them: He enlarges nations, then leads them away. He strips understanding from the leaders of the earth and makes them wander in a pathless waste. They grope in the dark without light, He makes them stagger like a drunkard.*

Job 12:23–25 NRSV

Have you ever wondered what God is going to do with all the nations, the tribes and the various mixtures we have become? How will He decide between the sheep and the goats?

What defines a sheep nation as opposed to a goat nation? How does God define them? What will happen to all those political borders we see on maps which have changed over the years? Do they matter at all? One look at a map more than a few years old will show how the borders have changed beyond belief. Which of the borders will God choose? Does God choose borders at all? After all He is not like us. What about the feelings of those current-day nations where various empires with their wars and ambitions have fought over tracts of land and where boundaries have been put, regardless of the feelings or ethnicity of the people living there? Where the border was placed there by important people in empires who maybe did not even care about the cultures, religion, or language of those who had to live with the consequences?

What about those nations like Belgium who have ended up with two strong languages spoken by her people, both needing to be heard? Two cultures who both need honouring? I am not even going to touch at this point the smaller minorities in the land or the fact that Belgium plays host on her territory to a massive governmental entity called the European Union. Are such nations legitimate? How does God deal with them? I am not so convinced we have all those answers yet.

In the meantime, I deeply honour the borders, leaders and the flags of others until God says otherwise. No matter how ugly or misguided that flag may be. I do not think I have seen a totally pure one yet. No matter how cruel or thoughtless a political border might be, we honour it until God says otherwise. No matter how great or small you feel the leader is. I also deeply honour those who have tried to bring the two sides of Belgium together. No easy task and way beyond any endeavour man might attempt. The stakes too are higher than any we might think in a small nation.

Well, Job had a try at explaining the mysterious ways of God to his would-be comforters. They may not have got it all right but this is not bad actually—just a pity about the unwelcome advice—but then I expect God had always wanted to surprise them with His answer at the end. He likes to do this! In these verses the word for nation is "goy", that is, a Gentile nation usually, or sometimes the nations who descend from Abraham, yet remain a heathen nation or people. God in His wisdom can either increase or decrease these nations then.

So then a good look at your Strong's Concordance here to get the message. God "makes nations great" *(saga)*, that is, He grows them, He magnifies them, He increases them. But just as suddenly He destroys them *(abad)*, that is, He breaks them, He causes them to be lost, to perish, to vanish. Wow!

God enlarges *(satah)* the nations, that is, He spreads out, He extends, He stretches out. Then He leads them away *(naha)*, He guides, He governs, He straightens—in the sense here of undoing the increase they have enjoyed. He does it despite all our efforts. He is not some cruel god who does things on whim like the gods of Greece or Rome who have to be placated to keep them from their random destructive tendencies. No, this is a God who moves on the hearts of men and women in leadership and whose involvement with them can bring favour or times of judgment.

All nations have leaders unless they are in really dire straits, whether they be kings, presidents, prime ministers or other roles. Let's hope the worst bits of these verses do not also apply to our spiritual leaders! It is not good when God causes this aimless wandering.

Again, the Hebrew is interesting. God literally "takes away the heart", that is, *leb*, the heart, the will, the understanding of the leaders of the earth. Not good in any nation. Here the peoples of the earth are *ammi*, compatriots, persons, peoples, kinsmen. They wander in a "pathless waste", they reel, they stray, they err in a wilderness, *tohu*, an empty space, a waste, a place without form. Compare this with Genesis where the earth is likewise "without form and void" until God comes with *His* light well in advance of the moon, sun and stars which do not arrive until the fourth day of creation. This wilderness means to wander without the light of God. Our understanding is darkened by the Almighty.

It seems all very pertinent for our nations at this moment in time where just about everything that can be shaken is being shaken. Please dwell on what God is *doing* in the darkness because His heart is always unto salvation and healing, always about calling forth His divine mandate to heal and deliver and restore. It is His very nature and His holy character. A second breath of life has to come and no human being can do this unless God is with him.

Ode to Joy?

At the Centre of it all.

Do you know this anthem? The words? They are well worth looking at. It is, of course, the anthem of the EU. Brussels, in Belgian heartland today, was chosen to be the governmental seat of the EU. Well, the words to the *Ode* were written in 1785 by Friedrich Schiller and set to music in the Ninth Symphony by Beethoven. It is the more peaceful part of the symphony, by the way, when the more turbulent noise of conflict music is overtaken by this song. It is meant to be used to express our desire for brotherhood and peace, to give hope in our battles for justice under oppression. The *Ode* is a bit heavy for my taste. Not to worry.

Did you know that, in the very beginning of Brussels, when there were islands where there is now solid ground and canals, a much-loved St Géry, bishop of Cambrai, settled himself on one of those islands and began to influence those around? A pity the yellow irises that grew there then have disappeared but the memory lives on in the emblem of Brussels. The bishop's character? Well, he was known by all for his joy. A sort of joyful, saintly, loving, wise, founding father at the founding of what would become the city of Brussels. I doubt he would recognise his island today. Coincidence? No. I think God always wanted to establish *His* character and *His* holy joy at the heart of the Belgian capital and at the heart of Europe. God is very serious about His joy. Of course it means we draw our very strength from it. Of course the enemy knows it too and will do it all to establish sheer misery and bloodshed or a humanistic type of joy and brotherhood which, at best, is partial and, at its worst, allows room for a more occult type of unity and peace to creep in. Still though, my mind drifts to the founder who had joy and I pray that his legacy will bear fruit today.

Again I ask: Have you ever so deeply loved a nation that you wanted to hold her and love her back to life? Some nations do that to your heart. Places are chosen for purpose, you know, even if they are covered with concrete for centuries. God never forgets His original plan and purpose.

A visit to the outlying area of Brussels shows how the past does indicate the mandate given of God for the future—if we will bow and accept. Here, in the lovely wooded area, a lovely friend and intercessor showed me where the royals of Europe would come to hunt and take counsel. A restful place. Interesting that the EU buildings are also here where current-day political kings do their best to take counsel.

No coincidence that this happens here. The area was marked out long ago for this purpose. The land has been given a mandate to bring counsel from a place of rest—for kings in the political and the spiritual realm. Little wonder then that Belgium is a monarchy and has a king called *King of the Belgians*. No wonder the enemy covets this land so much. A brief look at John van Ruysbroeck (1293–1381) is interesting.[1] That governmental calling of a much more spiritual leaning still has to be fulfilled. At Groenendael, near Brussels, he contemplated and taught on the divine union with Jesus. This teaching too needs grafting back into the spiritual picture that is Belgium, so as to bring healing to the nation.

Controversially, these Flemish were mystics but their role cannot be underestimated. They were kings and priests of a different kind. Hadewijch of Antwerp, Hildegard of Bingen and other visionaries have left a spiritual inheritance as important as the kings and rulers who reigned here and fought their battles here.

So what is God doing? He is preparing a remnant people who will pay a price in these times.

I believe we are in End Times and that this royal, priestly anointing is needed. The huge mandate I hear from the Lord for modern day Belgians who love Him is that they will rise up in an unprecedented royal, priestly calling and that, in this way, the grafting can happen. They will pay a huge price for this. They will fight, a small number maybe: they will be wounded warriors. The price cannot be underestimated. I think I never saw such a price in any other European nation. It will take an unprecedented healing, a holy desire that can only come from the Lord. This is for much more than Belgium—it is

---

1 His original Flemish name was Jan van Ruusbroec.

the healing of the tectonic plates of so many deep-seated wounds from empire wars as well as from ethnic conflicts as yet unresolved. All over Europe. Whether Belgium will survive intact at the end I do not know, but what I do know is that the sacrifices of those who fight in the Spirit realm will heal the hurts and the traumas of centuries. Just nobody is healed enough for that as yet. God allows time for that kind of healing.

A Selah pause—Some questions

"But Mary kept all these things, and pondered them in her heart."

Luke 2:19 NKJV

And the questions. Why so many battles on Belgian soil? Why so much bloodshed? Why was the future of European empires decided here? Why is there still a divide across the land?

Why, why, why? And then the thought that, just as battles of religion, and of empires, had been fought here—so here could great healing come. Healing in these bloody places can cause greater healing to come in many nations and places. It still has to happen.

A Divine Skin Graft

Your skin is an organ, right? It breathes, it feels, it responds to the touch of love or of hate. It matters as much as your heart or your lungs. Ask any victim of serious burns. Once I saw in the Spirit for Belgium a huge skin graft. You may have seen one although hopefully you never needed one in the natural.

Now I had a thought—which is not my own—that Belgium needs such a divine graft. Nations which are put together by others often do not feel good in their skin. This cannot be a natural thing at all. I saw how human efforts at doing this skin graft had failed—just as in the natural the skin of the recipient can reject the graft from another part of the body intended to heal the wound and persuade new fresh skin to grow. Spiritually there has been this shift in the tectonic plates and the grafting—even in the Body of Christ—has not worked at times. And these are very critical times we live in.

But God...

God has other plans well beyond our understanding. He can graft together two skins which are not alike so that true unity can be established. But there needs to be humility from both sides, accepting the wounds of the other. Because I believe I have heard that God intends that—despite the ambitious greed of humanity and our empires, despite the circumstances of history which left a modern nation with the problem of at least two languages and a maze of cultural differences— Belgium is to be one. The gift and calling is irrevocable. I believe this calling is spiritually legitimate. God permits so much turmoil and grief to bring out of it some leaders and kings who will come into their own destiny in dark times.

So once again: why Belgium? Why the battles here?

The first key is the strategic importance of Belgian territory in terms of its geography. Access to roads, rivers, trade routes, the sea, resources. This can cause empires to retain control over places they would not normally have an interest in. It can lead them to place borders where the ethnic patchwork of the land does not at all reflect the border imposed.

The second key is spiritual. Ancient pacts. I saw once in a vision some ancient tribes. Gallic tribes. Think of Caesar's Gallic Wars. These tribes absolutely would not surrender to Roman rule. Ambiorix and Vercingetorix fiercely resisted the invasion of their homelands.[2] I had once an astounding answer to my question of why the land was inviting war and bloodshed. With my spiritual eyes, I saw an ancient scene rise where Gallic warriors tore themselves with knives and their women shouted for them to go to war. They had dedicated themselves to war. And somehow it can still play itself out, centuries later. The desire for freedom is incredible but the pacts made with the bloody gods of war are still active if not retracted.

Trauma and the cry of the land

Of course some of these battles were fought on what used to be Belgian soil and is now part of surrounding nations. There are so many empires, duchies and nations concerned it's easy to lose count: Spain, Gallic tribes, France, England and Scotland, Austria, Holland...

Sambre 57 BC, Waterloo 1815, Ypres/Passchendaele 1917, Battle of the Bulge/Ardennes 1945.

---

2 Ambiorix was a prince of the Eburones, the leader of a Belgic tribe of north-eastern Gaul (Gallia Belgica) where modern Belgium is located. In the nineteenth century, Ambiorix became a Belgian national hero because of his resistance against Julius Caesar, as written in Caesar's *Gallic Wars*. For more information, see en.wikipedia.org/wiki/Ambiorix.

The creation waits in eager expectation for the revelation of the sons of God. For the creation was subjected to futility, not by its own will, but because of the One who subjected it, in hope that the creation itself will be set free from its bondage to decay and brought into the glorious freedom of the children of God.

Romans 8:19–21 BSB

Have you ever felt the land speak to you? No, of course I do not mean worship of the earth or any such thing. I mean when the pain of the land and the inner groanings of the people there, creation itself crying out in pain and then—amazingly—recognising your footprints as you pass.

Healing does not come easily, though, where the hurt is so deep. If you look with the eyes of your heart and listen with the ears of your heart, you will sense the deep desire of this land and her people to be healed and come into her destiny.

The deaths are beyond reckoning and no doubt thousands of bodies still lie under modern day cities and in the fields. And the blood cries out.

I wondered and wondered why all the battles seem to have taken place on what is now Belgian soil. Totally out of proportion to the size of the nation. You could say it is because of the strategic position of a nation, because of the fighting of empires and the ambitions of men. You could say many things but none of them totally explain the convergence of so many foreign armies on Belgian soil. Not just once—indeed once would have been quite enough—but many, many times over the centuries. Europe has fought to the death here and the land still remembers. There is such a thing as generational memory which affects us all.

Deep trauma affects the land and the people for many generations after the terrible events happened. Trauma gets stuffed down and forgotten. We prefer to forget. But God has his very own book of remembrance and when the time comes, he will cause prophetic people to recall, to remember and remind him of things that have been forgotten. Things forgotten about—good and bad—are waking up.

The years 2020 and 2021 so far are remembered for the battle against COVID. The coronavirus. A real war of crowns is going on in heavenly places.

> *Is Your steadfast love declared in the grave, or Your faithfulness in Abaddon? Are Your wonders known in the darkness or Your saving help in the place of forgetfulness?*

Psalm 88:11–12 ESV

The answer is 'yes'. The land is waking up. God remembers. His books are being revealed to us. May we remember too.

The Cry

1. A plain and a birth as a buffer zone

The Lord said, "What have you done? Listen! Your brother's blood cries out to Me from the ground."

Genesis 4:10 NLT

Do not pollute the land where you are. Bloodshed pollutes the land, and atonement cannot be made for the land on which blood has been shed, except by the blood of the one who shed it.

Numbers 35:33 NIV

Waterloo, Waterloo, Waterloo, morne plaine![1]

These words by Victor Hugo are well known by both the Belgians and the French, and are even taught in school in many European nations. They come from the very first verses of a poem describing what happened at the end of the Napoleonic wars, when the French emperor was finally defeated by the troops led by Wellington. This all happened in a little village in the countryside, not far away from Brussels, called Waterloo.

---

1 Waterloo! Waterloo! Waterloo! gloomy plain!
 In 1852, Victor Hugo wrote many versions for this verse that became quite famous in its final version:
 Waterloo! Waterloo! champ noir! tragique plaine! (black field, tragic plain)
 Waterloo! Waterloo! morne et tragique plaine! (gloomy and tragic plain)
 Waterloo! Waterloo! champ maudit! morne plaine! (cursed field)

45

Blood... blood... blood... rivers of blood in the plain.

The blood of thousands of young soldiers from all over Europe, who happened to be gathered in that plain that terrible day, when the armies of two great empires (England and France), joined by other superpowers (Prussia, Russia, Austria), clashed for supremacy. That was the birth context of what would later become Belgium, that little nation which has now become the host of so many European institutions in its capital, Brussels.

In Wikipedia, *History of Belgium*, we read "the birth of a nation" reported as follows:

> *After Napoleon's defeat at Waterloo in 1815, the major victorious powers (Britain, Austria, Prussia, and Russia) agreed at the Congress of Vienna on uniting the former Austrian Netherlands (Belgium Austriacum) and the former Seven United Provinces, creating the United Kingdom of the Netherlands, which was to serve as a buffer state against any future French invasions. This was under the rule of a Protestant king, William I. Most of the small and ecclesiastical states in the Holy Roman Empire were given to larger states at this time, and this included the Prince-Bishopric of Liège which now became formally part of the United Kingdom of the Netherlands.*

> *The enlightened despot William I, who reigned from 1815 to 1840, had almost unlimited constitutional power, the constitution having been written by a number of notable people chosen by him.*

Talk about a traumatic birth, talk about a cruel "fatum"—to be created as a "buffer zone" by one great kingdom (England) in order to protect itself from another great nation (France). And furthermore to be placed under the despotic power and authority of a third one (the Netherlands), and being given a name supposed to conjure unity: the United Kingdom of the Netherlands.

Well, in about fifteen years, this proclaimed unity would prove to be an illusion. A portion of the new little buffer state screamed and fought for independence and became free from the Netherlands as "Belgium", a new monarchy.

One can only wonder what would have happened had Wellington been defeated by Napoleon that day, and not the opposite. Would France have imposed its language on all the territory now called Belgium?

What if Napoleon had not been defeated? Would France have expanded and become the neighbouring country of the Netherlands, each country speaking its own language, with no need to be bilingual on the same little territory artificially created as a buffer?

The question can be asked; the answer only there to help us better understand the challenge for the people of the little buffer state, created from two pieces of territory where two different languages were spoken, in need now to find a way to live together, understand one another and function as one.

Not only were the French Empire, the British Empire and the Netherlands involved in the creation of the "buffer zone", but all the major powers of that time had a word to say about what this new little territory should become, as they all gathered together in Vienna to shape the territories and draw the boundaries of "Europe as we know and will know it" for projected future generations.

This Vienna Congress lasted very long—many months—with a great deal of money spent during it; Metternich from Austria was the diplomat who organised the discussions; Talleyrand entered the negotiations, although initially he had not been appointed to represent France. However he managed to gain access to the discussion table and represent French interests.

In 1815, it was not yet Belgium but "le royaume uni des Pays-Bas / het Koninkrijk der Nedelanden / the United Kingdom of the Netherlands" which was created. Belgium as a kingdom emerged in 1830 when the locals threw the Dutch out in an act of independence and rebellion against the Netherlands.

A German king, Leopold de Saxe Cobourg Gotha was chosen to become "King of the Belgians" *(Roi des Belges)*, not "King of Belgium" *(Roi de Belgique)*—king over *people*, not over a *territory*. He was also, some say,[2] a 32-degree freemason and would have been appointed Grand Master, had he not chosen to become king of the Belgians.

So began the history of "Belgium as we know it", politically, linguistically and spiritually speaking. Not many people are aware of this. Yet to understand Belgium, its heart, its

---

2 See chapter 5 of this book for more details.

struggles, its destiny, this "book of remembrance" has to be opened, read and spiritually understood. Now is the time.[3]

Since it was "for such a time as this" this little buffer zone in Europe has been created.

---

3 Historically, things are quite complicated: Belgium was not created as a buffer zone, but rather the United Kingdom of the Netherlands (1815); Belgium came to be by the revolt of the Belgians due to a wish for independence, against the strategy of the Vienna Congress.

2. A Congress and a treaty

Do not move your neighbour's boundary stone set up by your predecessors in the inheritance you receive in the land the Lord your God is giving you to possess.

Deuteronomy 19:14 NIV

After a battle on a plain around a small village called Waterloo, a Congress in the stately Austrian capital of Vienna was the next step towards the creation of Belgium. Again, Wikipedia helps us set the historic stage:[1]

The Congress of Vienna of 1814–1815 was one of the most important international conferences in European history. It remade Europe after the downfall of the French Emperor Napoleon I. It was a meeting of ambassadors of European states chaired by Austrian statesman Klemens von Metternich,[2] and held in Vienna... The objective was to provide a long-term peace plan for Europe by settling critical issues arising from the French Revolutionary Wars and the Napoleonic Wars. The goal was not simply to restore old boundaries but to resize the main powers so they could balance each other and remain at peace... France lost all its recent conquests while Prussia, Austria and Russia made major territorial gains...

---

1 See en.wikipedia.org/wiki/Congress_of_Vienna.
2 Klemens von Metternich was an Austrian diplomat who was at the centre of European affairs for three decades as the Austrian Empire's foreign minister.

The Congress's "final act" was signed nine days before Napoleon's final defeat at Waterloo on 18 June 1815... In a technical sense, the "Congress of Vienna" was not properly a congress: it never met in plenary session. Instead, most of the discussions occurred in informal, face-to-face sessions among the Great Powers of Austria, Britain, France, Russia, and sometimes Prussia, with limited or no participation by other delegates. On the other hand, the Congress was the first occasion in history where, on a continental scale, national representatives came together to formulate treaties instead of relying mostly on messages among the several capitals. The Congress of Vienna settlement formed the framework for European international politics until the outbreak of the First World War in 1914.

By reading this, one can understand that a kind of "bargaining" was taking place between the victors and against the defeated French Empire, with each trying to gain parts of territories and power.

Negotiations "behind closed doors" were happening; transparency and fair-play were not the main realities in this so-called congress. Delegates were not meeting in plenary sessions and the intention was not to restore old boundaries, but to "balance power". Such was the context of the creation of what would firstly be the "United Kingdom of the Nethelands", from which fifteen years later, in 1830, Belgium as we know it today, would emerge as a new nation.

The first "transplant" or "grafting" did not appear to work very well and, after only fifteen years, one part of the new artificial territory rejected the other and, in a need to affirm its own identity, determined to be quite the opposite of The Netherlands—for where The Netherlands was Protestant, the new kingdom of Belgium would be essentially Catholic and, for the ones really not devoted to Catholicism, freemason.[3]

So, first, from a deep wound—the bloody defeat in Waterloo—and, second, from a heart-felt rebellion against the perceived "oppressive power" of the Netherlands, Belgium was born. Not such an easy start in life...

One has to add here that, although Waterloo and the Vienna Congress went very far in this dismantling and re-assembling of territories, the boundaries of what is known today as Belgium had very often moved and merged throughout earlier centuries.

Also, what would become the line of separation between the French-speaking Walloons and the Dutch-speaking Flemish, namely, the line cutting through the central part of "future Belgium", had already been a major dividing line in former

---

3 See chapter 5 for further details. See also redalyc.org/jatsRepo/3695/369545832006/html/index.html. If "Belgian" freemasonry was a largely unproblematic social structure during the 18th century, it took a completely new direction in the first decades of the 19th. A set of new lodges with a mainly bourgeois membership gradually generated a freemasonry that was increasingly anticlerical and openly political as it became the backbone of the country's liberal party. This shift in freemasonry seems to have come through the French officers, who imported the more anticlerical freemasonry.

centuries: the famous "limes" or "Roman wall" that separated the Roman world from the Germanic one.[4]

So, the little territory that would soon become Belgium, had a serious challenge to meet: it had to unite in one nation two worlds, languages and cultures—that had been separated for centuries by a wall.

---

4 See the article "Le limes romain de Belgique" by Albert Grenier, *Journal des Savants*, Année 1944, 4, pp. 178–181, which states that "La limite des langues flamande et wallonne paraît correspondre, de manière assez exacte, à la frontière que s'était tracée l'empire romain au IVème siècle" or, in English, "The limit of the Flemish and Walloon languages seems to correspond, quite exactly, to the border drawn by the Roman Empire in the 4th century."

3. A Question: Can these bones live?

The hand of the Lord was upon me, and He brought me out by the Spirit of the Lord and set me in the middle of a valley; it was full of bones. He led me back and forth among them, and I saw a great many bones on the floor of the valley, bones that were very dry. He asked me, "Son of man, can these bones live?"

Ezekiel 37:1–3 NIV

And when I passed by you and saw you wallowing in your blood, I said to you in your blood, "Live!" I said to you in your blood, "Live!"

Ezekiel 16:6 ESV

From the first book of the Bible, from Genesis and the shedding of blood by Cain murdering his brother Abel, we know that "the blood cries out", that the earth itself is affected by the battles fought on its soil. In other passages of the Book, we even read that the earth is groaning.

What to expect then on a territory that is known as "the battlefield of Europe"?

In Waterloo, it is estimated that 23,700 people died, while 65,400 were wounded. Blood, shed. Bloodshed. The blood of a generation of young soldiers who came from many different nations of Europe. All shed on the soil of what would become Belgium. Historians consider that the four days of battle in Waterloo were a real butchery, one of the bloodiest incidents of the Napoleonian wars. Some write that, in one day, around 55,000 men were killed or severely wounded. Two thousand amputations would have taken place at Waterloo...

We understand better how a national poet such as Victor Hugo would have felt driven to write about this *"gloomy plain"*, trying to put some words on what must have been a national, and even international, trauma.

Some bodies were never retrieved. In fact, only one complete skeleton has been recovered from the battlefield, quite recently, in 2012, during archaeological excavations. The body remains appear to be those of a young man of twenty-three, from Hanover, who has been described as "the soldier of Waterloo". The bones are displayed in the *Waterloo Memorial 1815*, a museum built in 2015 on the ground of the battlefield.

One question here: *Why was only one complete skeleton found?*

The answer to this question is heart-breaking. Historian John Sadler states: *"Many who died that day in Waterloo were buried in shallow graves but their bodies were later disinterred and their skeletons taken. They were ground down and used as fertiliser and taken back home to be used on English crops."*[1]

Bodies ground down and used as fertiliser on the victor's ground...

---

1 See Barney White-Spunner, *Of Living Valour: The Story of the Soldiers of Waterloo*, Simon & Schuster UK 2015.

No honour shown to the dead.

Even a form of desecration, as human bodies would be used to enrich crops and food...

Another question: what about the "Waterloo teeth"? Have you ever heard about them?

I did, whilst in preparation for writing of this book. The "Waterloo teeth" were taken from the dead bodies of soldiers after the battle, and made into dentures. The British Dental Association explains: *"False teeth could be carved from hippopotamus, walrus, or elephant ivory, but these looked less real and rotted more quickly than human teeth. Human corpses were the best source of replacement teeth. After a major battle, like the one at Waterloo in 1815, scavengers would scour the field with pliers, ready to loot the mouths of dead soldiers."*

These teeth were guaranteed to have come from young, healthy soldiers, men killed in the prime of life...

Selah. Take a pause.
Take a deep breath.
Dare to feel it.
Think of it.

But we're not done yet.

Not only did thousands of men die in Waterloo, but it is also estimated that 7,000 horses died in battle. What do we learn about those horses?

Dead horses had their metal shoes ripped off for re-selling before being arranged in vast pyres and set alight. The scene was made even more hellish by the stacks of unburied human bodies that lay around for days afterwards, literally going black in the scorching heat of the June sun. The only thing to do was burn the men just as they did the horses— according to one source, "they have been obliged to burn upwards of a thousand carcasses, an awful holocaust to the War-Demon."[2]

What can the effects of such butchery be?

Can some lasting effects remain on the plain or its surroundings?

What are the consequences on the next generations, the sons, the grandsons, the great- and great-great-grandsons of the ones who survived, often maimed?

For many years, Belgium has had a gloomy reputation in Christian international circles. It has been known as "the graveyard of missionaries". The expression was repeated, broadly—fame and shame were combined. Some missionaries would come, with a calling and the desire to share the Good News, yet, after some years of faithfully "ploughing the ground", would have to retreat, leaving Belgium, with little fruit for their toil. Stony ground, where the seed did not take root...

Also, for many years, missionaries and evangelists shared the heaviness they felt when landing at Brussels National

---

2 Extract from the article "Five grisly facts about the battle of Waterloo", published on the blog of Yesterday UK TV.

Airport; the impression of dark clouds surrounding the place and making for a heavy atmosphere.

Another aspect: according to official statistics, Belgium has had, for many years, the highest suicide rate of any West-European country. The Belgian suicide rate is even "dismally high", according to WHO, the World Health Organisation.[3] "Suicidal behaviours (thoughts, attempts, and actual suicides) represent an important problem for public health and society in Belgium" is what we can read on the official website of the Belgian government.[4]

Christian intercessors in Belgium have not been inactive during the recent past, however, and fortunately things have begun to change. For some years now, the same visitors, when landing at the national airport, report having had other impressions: they have seen breakthroughs of light (holes) through the clouds and they've felt that the lid of spiritual heaviness has begun to lift.

Also, for the first time in many years, in 2018, the suicide rate of Belgium began to decrease.[5]

Some, with prophetic vision, began to proclaim: *"Belgium, arise!"*

We want to join in this proclamation.

---

3 www.thebulletin.be/belgian-suicide-rate-dismally-high-according-who.
4 www.healthybelgium.be/en/health-status/mental-health/suicidal-behaviour.
5 Now, with the COVID-19 pandemic and the resulting lockdown, the situation is detoriorating again, but, yet, a "passing of the peak" could be observed before this crisis.

Yet, to help this come about, account must be taken of unresolved pain and iniquities: confession, repentance, last pushes and intercessory prayer are needed.

Let us not take deep wounds lightly. Let us remember what Jeremiah, the so-called "weeping prophet", wrote:

> ...*They dress the wound of My people as though it were not serious. "Peace, peace," they say, when there is no peace.*

Jeremiah 6:14 NIV

> *For the brokenness of the daughter of my people I am crushed. I mourn; horror has gripped me. Is there no balm in Gilead? Is no physician there? Why then has the health of the daughter of my people not been restored?*

Jeremiah 8:21–22 BSB

Let us consider what repetitive traumas—from birth pangs to multiple bloodbaths—do to a person and to a people. Let us not try to heal them lightly, saying "peace peace" when in fact, the balm has not been applied in depth.

May this book help us remember in order to attend to the wounds; let it be one of the means to help see *Beautiful Belgium* come forth and shine.[6]

---

6 See Appendix 1 written by Jean-Antoine, at the end of this book.

The Challenge

4. An Austrian diplomat

Deceitful speech is reprehensible to the Lord, but those who act faithfully are His delight.

Proverbs 12:22 ISV

The people of the Levi tribe will speak each curse in a loud voice, then the rest of the people will agree to that curse by saying, "Amen!" Here are the curses: We ask the Lord to put a curse on anyone who moves the rocks that mark property lines...

Deuteronomy 27:16–18 CEV

Diplomacy.

It can be a compliment, when we refer to a "sense of diplomacy" in someone—meaning that a person knows what to say and how to say it without damaging the relationship by causing offence.

Yet, diplomacy can also have a "sharp edge". According to the Encyclopedia Britannica, diplomacy is the practice of influencing the decisions and conduct of foreign governments or organisations through dialogue, negotiation, and other nonviolent means.

This last part attracts our attention: the "other nonviolent means". Presented as "other means", yet not defined.

Diplomacy is what happened before and after the battle of Waterloo. And it happened on other territory, far from the battleground, in the capital of Austria: Vienna. Here is what we can read[1] about the Congress of Vienna:

The Congress functioned through formal meetings such as working groups and official diplomatic functions; however, a large portion of the Congress was conducted informally at salons, banquets, and balls.

Virtually every state in Europe had a delegation in Vienna—more than 200 states and princely houses were represented at the Congress. In addition, there were representatives of cities, corporations, religious organisations (for instance, abbeys) and special interest groups… The Congress was noted for its lavish entertainment: according to a famous joke it did not move, but danced.

Klemens Wenzel, Prince von Metternich was an Austrian politician. He is thought of as one of the most important diplomats of all time. Metternich was Foreign Minister for Austria… After the Napoleonian defeat, he believed that the best way to keep Europe peaceful was to create a balance of power, which means that no country is strong enough to beat all the other countries. To make sure this happened, he made some countries stronger, so that other countries (especially France) would have to think twice about going to war.

Beyond pointing the finger at the obvious ones involved (England, Austria, Prussia), there seems to have been a hidden agenda behind smoke screens. As a large portion of the

---

1 en.wikipedia.org/wiki/Congress_of_Vienna.

Congress was conducted informally at salons, banquets, and balls, a lot of room was given to the use of "other nonviolent means" of diplomacy.

The weird hidden agenda was probably the reason for the weird alliance between Catholics and liberals in order to create "Belgium". Many promises seem to have been made behind the scenes;[2] very few people were aware of those promises made at the time of the creation of Belgium. The people who made the promises did not necessarily have the rightful authority or legal position to do so.

Some did it out of greed and craving for power, operating out of what we call a "seductive spirit". Indeed, historically, it seems that Metternich functioned very much through whispers in the ear, whispering promises with nothing put on paper ("bouche à oreille", as the French say).

Much money and many financial interests were at stake too.

According to the Rothschilds' archives,[3] in 1820, Prince Metternich, Austrian Minister for Foreign Affairs, entered into negotiations with the House of Rothschild for a large loan. The complicated arrangements for this enormous loan

---

2 This part, expanding on what the use of the "other nonviolent means" can have been, is inpired by a time of intercession I had with a few spiritual leaders from different countries following the National Day of Prayer 2020; during this time, someone saw sealed scrolls handed over behind the scenes—which indeed, given the "dancing context" of the Congress, could have happened.

3 From family.rothschildarchive.org/people/24-salomon-mayer-von-rothschild-1774-1855.

demanded the presence of a Rothschild in Vienna and thus Salomon Rothschild moved to the city and established a bank there.

Some writers claim that, as Nathan Mayer Rothschild had early knowledge of the outcome of the Battle of Waterloo, his couriers would have delivered information about the victory back to London before even the British Cabinet itself knew. It is thought he used this knowledge to speculate on the London Stock Exchange and make a vast fortune through an unfair advantage over other British stock holders, essentially defrauding them.

Anyway, something that is factual is that, in 1816, his four brothers were raised to the nobility by the Emperor of Austria. They were now permitted to prefix the Rothschild name with the particle 'von'.

This is to say that the coming into existence of Belgium in 1830 was very much the result, not only of an official gathering of nations to discuss the best possible future for Europe after a bloody war, but also the result of less transparent transactions by parties less directly identified as official stakeholders.

Or, to say it with less diplomacy: much bargaining and manouvering took place around the birth of baby Belgium!

5. A German king and master

The king's heart is in the hand of the Lord, as the rivers of water: He turns it whithersoever He will. Every way of a man is right in his own eyes: but the Lord ponders the hearts.

Proverbs 21:1–2 KJV

As Ignace Demaerel, leader of the movement Pray4Belgium, reminded me recently, Belgium was not born all "at once".

First, what was created in 1815 at the Congress of Vienna was an entity that was called the *United Kingdom of the Netherlands*, which was to serve as a buffer state against any future French invasions. The "United Netherlands" was created in the aftermath of the Napoleonic Wars through the fusion of territories that had belonged to other nations or entities. It was created as a constitutional monarchy, ruled by William I of the House of Orange-Nassau.

This political entity collapsed after only fifteen years, in 1830, with the outbreak of the Belgian Revolution. With the defacto secession of Belgium, the Netherlands was left with a reduced territory. It refused to recognise Belgian independence until 1839 when the Treaty of London was signed, fixing the border between the two states and guaranteeing Belgian independence and neutrality as the "Kingdom of Belgium".[1]

---

1 See for more details en.wikipedia.org/wiki/United_Kingdom_of_the_ Netherlands.

So, following a traumatic war, Belgium was born as the result of a rebellion and revolution to achieve independence and, we could say, to readjust its borders according to better "national feeling".

As a result of this rebellion, the new Kingdom of Belgium determined itself a lot as "contra".

Contra the Dutch and their Protestant king: the first government of Belgium would be a mixture of Catholics and freemasons (almost perfectly half/half). Indeed, the main political parties of the 19th century in Belgium were the Liberal Party and the Catholic—this first party being liberal not only in its economic views, but also in its religious/philosophical views.

This would later be reflected in the educational structures of the land, with the creation in 1834 of the ULB,[2] Université Libre de Bruxelles or Free University Brussels, "free" as in freemasonry.[3] The creators of this new university, which would present an alternative, contra, to the UCL,[4] were indeed freemasons.[5]

---

2 About this "freedom", see the book by Otto Bixler from Ellel Ministries, *It Isn't Free and It Isn't Masonry*, June 2016, Zaccmedia.

3 To bring some more nuance: freemasons in that time often were Catholic at the same time; it is only around 1838 the pope wrote an official letter condemning freemasonry, showing that these two were incompatible; so, in these years "freemason" did *not* mean "atheist".

4 Catholic University of Leuven, one of the oldest universities in Europe.

5 ULB and UCL are still the main French speaking universities in Belgium. Think of it: if you want to study in this country, you have to choose between a Catholic or a freemason university. Not such an easy choice.

Another expression of the "contra" would be in the choice of a king and an official language for the new Kingdom of Belgium. As the Orange-Nassau family and the Dutch had been discarded, the Belgian Revolution first led, in 1830, to the establishment of a Catholic and bourgeois, officially French-speaking and neutral, independent Belgium under a provisional government.[6] French was originally the single official language adopted by the nobility and the bourgeoisie. However it progressively lost its overall importance as Dutch also became recognised. This recognition became official only in 1898.[7]

Now a king had to be found for the new kingdom, and this took a bit of time. There were not that many suitable candidates; finally, the Belgian government offered the position to Leopold of Saxe-Cobourg-Gotha, who then became Leopold I of Belgium. What made him a suitable choice?

After Napoleon's defeat, Leopold had moved to the United Kingdom where he married Princess Charlotte of Wales, who was second in line to the British throne. He was offered the position because of his connections with royal houses across Europe, and because, as the British-backed candidate, he was not affiliated with other powers, such as France, which were believed to still have territorial ambitions in Belgium.[8]

---

6 For more information about the birth of Belgium, see en.wikipedia.org/wiki/Belgium.

7 And in 1967 (only), the parliament accepted a Dutch version of the Constitution.

8 For more information about Leopold I, see en.wikipedia.org/wiki/Leopold_I_of_Belgium.

As a German, Leopold of Saxe-Cobourg-Gotha was a Protestant. Yet, it appears that he was also a freemason. And not of a low degree, either: he would have been offered the post of *Serenest Grand Master of the New Lodge of the Grand Orient of Belgium*, which he would have declined and given to one of his closest collaborators.

The conditional "would have" is used here, as Belgian historians have engaged, through the years, in conflicting arguments about this.[9]

What is well established is that the birth of the kingdom of Belgium led in 1833 to the creation of the Grand Orient of Belgium.[10] What is less established is that its creation would have taken place with the support of Leopold I of Belgium, who would himself have been initiated in the "Loge l'Espérance" at Berne in 1813. And that he would have been offered the post of Serenest Grand Master.

This being said, an interesting fact about Leopold of Saxe-Cobourg-Gotha is that, once proclaimed king, he decided to attend services of the Protestant chapel close to the Coudenberg palace in the centre of Brussels. The chapel became the "Royal Chapel".[11] Yet the chapel is part of the Palace of Charles of Lorraine, friend of the French

---

9 See about this question Jean van Win, *Léopold Ier, le roi franc-maçon.*

10 A cupola of masonic lodges, accessible only to men, and which, like other continental European jurisdictions, did not require initiates to believe in a Supreme Being.

11 After the French Revolution, Napoleon had signed a decree assigning the chapel to the Protestant faith in October 1804.

philosopher Voltaire, well-known as a freemason. Here is what the official tourist website *visit.brussels* says about Charles and his palace:

The objects on display illustrate the life of aristocrats in the Austrian Netherlands and at the court of Brussels in the 18th Century: sedans, medals, china and silverware, clocks, Masonic objects... Charles of Lorraine was the governor of the Austrian Netherlands from 1744 to 1780, an intellectual, curious about science, and a connoisseur of Diderot and d'Alembert's encyclopedia. He was interested in occultism, an art lover, and a passionate collector.[12]

Why take time here to mention these aspects? Well, if the first King of the Belgians was a freemason of one of the highest degrees, to the point that he would have been offered the post of Grand Master of the new lodge of the new-born country, and if his Protestantism was of a nature expressing itself in a building with a masonic background, there are consequences for the spiritual development of the country.

Is this widely enough known ?

And if so, has it been confessed and repented of properly and by the right people?[13]

---

12 visit.brussels/en/place/Palace-of-Charles-of-Lorraine.

13 I myself attended the Protestant Royal Chapel of Brussels for ten years as a young nominal Protestant. When I later on was "born again" and no longer just a nominal Christian, I was clearly led to leave this chapel and begin anew, find and join another church, under Holy Spirit's guidance. And repent for having worshipped at a "mixed altar".

We know that freemasonry in a family can have as consequences early deaths, sterility, suicides (particularly for the firstborn males). What about the effects of freemasonry on a country? When the first king and "father of the land" is a prominent freemason?[14] Could that have anything to do with the high rate of suicides of Belgium? And if so, what should be done?

About the death of the firstborn son as a consequence of masonic covenants (especially for the highest degrees), it is interesting to notice what happened with the sons of Leopold I and Leopold II.

Leopold II was born in Brussels as the second but eldest surviving son of Leopold I. He succeeded his father to the Belgian throne and reigned for 44 years until his death (the longest reign of any Belgian monarch). He died without surviving legitimate sons.

The current Belgian king descends from his nephew and successor, Albert I. Leopold II's son had already died. When, however, Albert's older brother, Prince Baudouin of Belgium—who had subsequently been prepared for the throne—also died at an early age, Albert, at the age of 16, unexpectedly became second in line (after his father) to the Belgian Crown.

If a tree is known by its fruits, let us see here that the family tree, with the early death of the firstborn sons, points in the direction of freemasonry.

---

14 See the book by Otto Bixler, from Ellel Ministries, *Widows, Orphans and Prisoners*, January 2009, New Generations Publisher.

6. Reproducing the abuse: Congo

To do justice and judgment is more acceptable to the Lord than sacrifice. A haughty look, and a proud heart, and the plowing of the wicked, is sin... The getting of treasures by a lying tongue is a vanity tossed to and fro of them that seek death... Whoso stops his ears at the cry of the poor, he also shall cry himself, but shall not be heard.

Proverbs 21:3, 4, 6, 13 KJV21

Every monarchy, I suppose, has its good and bad kings. Certainly, Belgium has had good kings, like King Albert I for instance, who distinguished himself during World War I (see chapter 9 of this book) and was known as the "Knight-King".

Yet Leopold II, son of the first King of the Belgians and a first cousin of Queen Victoria of Britain, was "the best and the worst king" at the same time or, depending on your point of view, one or the other.

Leopold II is known as the Builder-King; most of the great avenues and parks in Brussels were built during his reign.[1] He

---

1 Such as the monumental *Arcade du Cinquantenaire* in Brussels.

played a significant role in the development of the modern Belgian state and made it economically prosperous. Yet this prosperity was built on the abuse of another nation: the Congo, which first became Leopold's personal property and, much later, a Belgian colony—this in itself was already quite a peculiar "montage".

If Belgium had been established as a buffer zone, artificially and for the benefit and peace of other nations, on bloodstained ground, the young nation would soon reproduce this pattern of using the bounty of others for one's own advantage. Born as the result of the Napoleonic war and trauma, abused or at least taken advantage of,[2] Belgium would in a certain sense reproduce the abuse on a "daughter nation", or rather, a colony.

Psychology has taught us over the last decades that unhealed trauma tends to duplicate itself. We see this for instance with paedophiles: often, they were themselves victims of paedophiles as children and, in the absence of proper help, tend as adults to become perpetrators and victimise others in the same fashion. The same is true with battered children, often the victims of parents who themselves, as children, had been bruised and battered by their own parents. An unending vicious circle that needs breaking.

---

2 If we want to use a vivid image to try to illustrate what being used as a buffer by others could mean, think of a mother and a father fighting with one another and the mother, at one point, putting her son or daughter between herself and her husband, as a shield. The child would then receive the punch, leaving both parents uninjured (we wouldn't dare say "at peace"). Buffer zones speak indeed more of "peace-seeking" than of true peace-making. In fact, war is not really far away. The buffer is there to be used in case it should erupt once again.

"As with human beings, so with nations"—says a Belgian intercessor active in inner healing for many years.[3]

Keen on establishing Belgium as an imperial power, Leopold II led the first European efforts to develop the Congo River basin.[4] He persuaded first the United States and then all the major nations of western Europe to recognise the Congo as his personal property. He called it *État Indépendant du Congo*, the "Congo Free State".[5] It was the world's only private colony, and Leopold referred to himself as its "proprietor".

Leopold's administration of the Congo Free State and its forced-labour system in the rubber industry were characterised by atrocities, including torture and murder, resulting from notorious systematic brutality. In 1890, George Washington Williams coined the term "crimes against humanity" to describe the practices of Leopold's administration in the Congo. The hands of men, women, and children were amputated when the quota of rubber was not met and millions of the Congolese people died.[6]

In his excellent book, *Congo. The Epic History of a People*,[7] David Van Reybrouck, a contemporary Belgian historian,

---

3 See the appendix at the end of this book about *Birth Trauma*.

4 About Leopold II, see britannica.com/biography/Leopold-II-king-of-Belgium.

5 Again, this vision of "freedom" is "one of its kind"—quite cynical towards the populations who would end up being treated as slaves.

6 See en.wikipedia.org/wiki/Leopold_II_of_Belgium.

7 See David Van Reybrouck's excellent book *Congo. Une histoire*, translated into English as *Congo. The Epic History of a People*, www.davidvanreybrouck.be.

depicts the situation: John Boyd Dunlop's invention of the inflatable rubber tyre created a demand for Congolese rubber. The profits went to build Belgium at the cost of Congolese lives. Murder was casual. Since bullets were in short supply, there was a habit of cutting off the hands of those who had been shot as proof a bullet had been used to shoot a person and not an animal. It was worse than slavery: "For while an owner took care of his slave... Leopold's rubber policies by definition had no regard for the individual." It would be absurd to talk of genocide or a holocaust, Van Reybrouck says, "but it was definitely a hecatomb."

Sadly enough, whereas Belgium had had to endure many atrocitities on its own territory at the Battle of Waterloo, it ended up reproducing atrocities in its colony, the Congo. This amputation of hands and feet is broadly documented in a book that, when published in 1998, became a best-seller: *Leopold's Phantom*.[8] The title is adopted from the 1914 poem, *The Congo*, by Illinois poet Vachel Lindsay. Condemning Leopold's actions, Lindsay wrote:

> *Listen to the yell of Leopold's ghost,*
> *Burning in Hell for his hand-maimed host.*
> *Hear how the demons chuckle and yell,*
> *Cutting his hands off, down in Hell.*

---

8 *King Leopold's Ghost: A Story of Greed, Terror and Heroism in Colonial Africa* (1998) is a best-selling popular history book by Adam Hochschild. The book was refused by nine of the ten U.S. publishing houses to which an outline was submitted, but became an unexpected bestseller. By 2013 more than 600,000 copies were in print in a dozen languages.

Already one century before the publishing of that book, Joseph Conrad had given a searing picture of the brutal and voracious European quest for Congo ivory in his novel *Heart of Darkness*. Conrad had spent six months in the Congo in 1890 as a steamboat officer.[9]

"Kurtz" is a central fictional character in this novel; a trader of ivory in Africa and commander of a trading post, who monopolises his position as a demigod among native Africans. If you remember Francis Ford Coppola's acclaimed 1979 Vietnam War film *Apocalypse Now*, it focuses on the protagonist's mission to find and kill the renegade "Colonel Kurtz", played by Marlon Brando and based on Conrad's character. The script acknowledges *Heart of Darkness* as a source of inspiration, and the last words of Colonel Kurtz, "The horror! The horror!" echo those of his namesake in the novel.

Butchery, again. Bloodshed, again.

Hell, heart of darkness, crime against humanity.

The role played in this bloodshed by Henri Morton Stanley, the Welsh-American journalist, explorer and later colonial administrator, who was famous for his exploration of central Africa and his search for missionary and explorer David Livingstone, should not be forgotten.

---

9 Conrad had a well-known penchant for teenage girls, and, when he was aged 65, he began a liaison with a teenager who was a former prostitute. She bore him two additional illegitimate children.

Stanley's book describing his journey, *Through The Dark Continent*, was a great success. One of those who read it was King Leopold II. The untamed land Stanley described sounded, to the Belgian king, like an ideal candidate for his colonial ambitions. Stanley had been trying to persuade the British authorities to commission him to bring the region under their control, but without success.

In 1879 Stanley led an expedition though the Congo basin for King Leopold, building roads, establishing steamship ports on the river, and persuading native rulers to sign away their rights to their lands. Even by the standard of his time Stanley was considered brutal—shooting natives for the the smallest provocation, looting stores of ivory, and giving people a foretaste of the new bloody regime.[10]

The history of Belgium and its colonies is not a glorious one. Honour has failed.

With respect to Rwanda and Burundi, they had been under Belgian administration for many years. When the horrible chapter of the genocide happened, thirty years after their independence, Belgium was not faultless. The former Belgian

---

10 For more information on this, read headstuff.org/culture/ history/henry-stanley-the-man-who-stole-the-congo/ or, in French, curieuseshistoires-belgique.be/henry-morton-stanley-le-conquistador-deprave. All this did not prevent this cruel tyrant from being knighted in 1899 and serving in the British Parliament from 1895 to 1900. But colonial history is today being reassessed and some of the so-called great men of past centuries are falling from their pedestals. See for instance the article published in The Independent, *The disfigured statue of Henry Morton Stanley we presume.*

rule had strengthened the division between both tribes—Hutus and Tutsis. Even if Belgium, during the genocide, was not directly involved in the killing, it failed to take responsibility and give proper assistance in times of extreme emergency. If colonies can be considered somehow as "daughter nations", Belgium failed as a mother.

Yet again, through the years, intercessors in Belgium have not been inactive. Many meetings have been organised between Christians from Belgium, the Congo, Rwanda and Burundi, to listen to testimonies, weep, repent, ask for and receive forgiveness and some healing. Letters have been written to the Government. Christian delegations went to the Congo to publicly ask forgiveness in 2006 and 2008. Intercessors and some church leaders did this, but it should also happen officially at governmental level. Such a form of administration and forced-labour system go deep into the make-up of a nation. Repenting must happen at a higher or deeper level.

A measure of deeper healing took place with the regrets personally expressed by King Philippe of Belgium. On 30 June 2020, on the 60th anniversary of the Congo's independence from Belgium, the monarch issued a statement expressing his "profound regret" for the wounds of the colonial past, and the "acts of violence and cruelty [that] were committed" in the Congo under Belgian occupation. A formal apology was not an option as that would require a political consensus. That's why the letter was drafted in his personal capacity, even though it had political backing from the prime minister.

Albeit this is clearly a step in the right direction, certain Congolese officials have said that an official asking of forgiveness still has to take place and, above all, some "righting of the wrong".[11]

---

11 See politico.eu/article/belgian-royals-remain-cautious-about-colonial-apology and africanews.com/ 2020/07/01/congolese-want-more-than-apology-for-belgium-s-colonial-impunity.

7. A place of gathering for kings

By Me kings reign, and rulers decree justice.

Proverbs 8:15 NKJV

Through the ages, what would one day become Belgium and "a buffer zone for Europe" has always been a territory where different nations and kings have gathered or collided.

If we look at the word itself, *"Belgium"*, the first mention of it appears in antiquity, when Julius Caesar writes in his book *De Bello Gallic*o that: "Of all these, the Belgians are the bravest."[1] The reason for this (less often quoted) is that they are "rude, barbarian", not well-refined.[2]

The Belgae were the inhabitants of the northernmost part of Gaul, which was significantly bigger than modern day Belgium. "Gallia Belgica", as it was commonly called, became a Roman province as a result of Caesar's conquests. Areas closer to the Rhine frontier, including the eastern part of

---

1 "Horum omnium fortissimi sunt Belgae", in Latin

2 For the etymology of the name Belgium/Belgians, see fr.wikipedia. org › wiki › Belges. A hypothetical link with Belenos/Bel is made there. See also, in the historic centre of Brussels, "La Maison de la Bellone", Bellone being a Roman goddess of war: fr.wikipedia.org/wiki/La_ Bellone.

modern Belgium, eventually became part of the province of "Germania Inferior", which interacted with Germanic tribes outside the empire.

This shows how the Germanic and Roman worlds, with their separate cultures and languages, already cohabited on this same territory, many centuries before Belgium as we know it was born.

In the Middle Ages, the Treaty of Verdun in the year 843 divided the Carolingian Empire into three kingdoms; most of modern Belgium was in the Middle Kingdom, later known as Lotharingia (from its ruler, Lothaire). "Louis le Germanique" was Lothaire's brother, occupying the neighbouring territory where, as the name of Louis indicates, the language spoken was German. Again, we see how "different tribes and tongues" were co-habiting on the map.

But the most interesting chapter for our region would happen a few centuries later, with the famous "Burgundians". At that time, in the 14th and 15th centuries, the Habsburg (from Austria) were reigning in a unified territory called "the Burgundian Netherlands" or "Duchy of Burgundy". At its height, roughly from 1350–1450, the Duchy spanned large parts of France and most of what is now Belgium and The Netherlands.

This relatively short period of "The Burgundians", covering less than a century, lies at the turning point between the Middle Ages and the Renaissance. These were happy, relatively peaceful times for the period, which saw prodigious advances in the fields of art and economics.[3] Unusually for the time, it was judicious marriages rather than wars that made the Burgundians strong.

In his 2019 book *The Burgundians*, told against the background of the Hundred Years' War and the constantly shifting alliances with France and England, Flemish writer Bart Van Loo[4] tells the story of the Burgundian elite and its remarkable court and culture. The title of the French translation, *Les Téméraires*, is a good choice for, in the 15th century, the term "Burgundy" designated a very large territory (much larger than present day Bourgogne) that almost became a new kingdom between France and Germany.

The period of "The Burgundians" was like a Golden Age, when the arts were flourishing, as well as spirituality. Major "Belgian" artists emerged, thanks to the patronage of the Dukes, particularly Philip the Good, who habitually resided at his palace in Brussels.[5] It is during that period that a movement called "the Flemish mystics" emerged, that had a wide influence throughout Europe.

---

3 For more information about this period, see focusonbelgium.be/en/facts/belgium-sauce-bourguignonne.

4 Bart Van Loo, *The Burgundians. A Vanished Empire.* Originally written and published in Flemish/ Dutch (2019). Translated and published in French in 2020: *Les Téméraires. Quand la Belgique défiait l'Europe, Bart Van Loo.* A publishing phenomenon in Europe, where it has sold 230,000 copies in hardback.

5 He also founded the University of Leuven (in 1425) and created the well-known *Order of the Golden Fleece.*

John van Ruysbroeck[6] (1293–1381) was an Augustinian canon and one of the most important of the Flemish mystics. Some of his main literary works include *The Kingdom of the Divine Lovers, The Twelve Beguines, The Spiritual Espousals, A Mirror of Eternal Blessedness, The Little Book of Enlightenment* and *The Sparkling Stone.*

He wrote in the Dutch vernacular, the language of the common people, rather than in Latin, the language of the Catholic Church liturgy and official texts, in order to reach a wider audience. He served as a parish priest at St. Gudula in Brussels and lived a life of extreme austerity. Later on, the desire for a more secluded lifestyle led Ruysbroeck to leave Brussels for the hermitage of Groenendaal, in the neighbouring Sonian Forest. The ruins of the monastery are still present in the forest of Soignes.

Due to his influence, many disciples joined the hermitage necessitating its transformation into a community which eventually became the motherhouse of a congregation. Ruysbroeck was appointed prior. During this time, his fame as a man of God, as a sublime contemplative and a skilled director of souls, spread beyond the bounds of Flanders and Brabant to Holland, Germany, and France.

Yet Ruysbroeck was not the first holy man to leave a spiritual imprint on Belgian soil. Before him, Bishop Géry, whose name is a shortened form of Gaudericus, is credited to have played a role in the birth of

---

6   His Flemish name is Jan van Ruusbroec.

Brussels as a city. Born to Roman parents, Géry was entrusted with the pastoral care of the city of Cambrai—hence his name, Géry of Cambrai—and later founded churches and abbeys in different places. Around the year 580, Gaudericus is said to have built a chapel on the largest island in the Senne near Brussels. Saint-Géry Island[7] is named after him. The man was known for radiating joy (hence his name, so some say, of Gaudericus, since *gaudium* in Latin means "joy").

Bishop Géry devoted himself to fighting paganism (he destroyed statues of idols), healing the sick (mainly lepers and people suffering from skin diseases) and setting the captives free, both in the natural (freeing slaves) and in the spiritual (delivering people oppressed by demons).[8]

One legend relates how he is supposed to have killed a dragon in Brussels.[9]

---

7 Quartier Saint-Géry in French, located in the centre of Brussels, colourful and full of restaurants and terraces where, in normal times, hundreds love to gather.

8 He went on a pilgrimage to visit the tomb of Sint-Martin of Tours and participated in the Concile of Paris in the year 614.

9 According to legend Géry erected a chapel (to Saint Michael, later Saints-Michel-et-Gudule cathedral), which soon became a church and gave birth to the city of Brussels from which he had chased a dragon whose lair was located there where the *Impasse du Dragon* was subsequently built, today renamed *Impasse de la Poupée*. See for more information, in French, Victor Devogel, *Légendes bruxelloises*, illustrations by C.-J. Van Landuyt, Brussels. See page 34: "A dragon was devastating Brussels, its countryside, its woods and its marshes. Some even claim that the Alley of the Dragon, which once existed in our city, got its name from the stay made there by this fabulous animal."

Spiritually speaking, this is not a trivial thing ("ce n'est pas rien", we would say in French), and we will come back to this in the third part of the book.

We can conclude here at the end of this chapter, that, throughout history, various nations, kings and leaders, both natural and spiritual leaders, have habitually gathered on the soil of what would subsequently become Belgium. Brussels was often their seat of government. Although empires came and went, the capital or administrative city often remained the same.

Depending on the century and ruling powers, this gathering of leaders and kings on our soil has been for better or worse.

The relatively happy and peaceful times of the Burgundians ended with the coming to power of Charles the Fifth (Carolus Quintus). Emperor Charles V, who was born in Belgium (Ghent), was the heir of the Dukes of Burgundy, and also of the royal families of Austria, Castile and Aragon. His presence and reign on our territory, as also that of his son Philip II of Spain was one of the gloomiest of our history.

8. Defying an Empire and embracing Reformation

"Put your sword back in its place," Jesus said to him, "for all who draw the sword will die by the sword."

Matthew 26:52 NIV

You shall not take the name of the Lord your God in vain [that is, irreverently, in false affirmations or in ways that impugn the character of God]; for the Lord will not hold guiltless nor leave unpunished the one who takes His name in vain [disregarding its reverence and its power].

Exodus 20:7 AMP

Amongst all the wars that can happen and have happened, wars of religion are amongst the ugliest. They happen in God's name: "Gott mit uns"—*God with us*—as Nazi Germany would claim centuries later. Well, when both camps claim God is at their side... that makes "God" seem like a very schizophrenic being. It dishonours His Name and the ones doing this could very well find themselves under the condemnation of having used God's Name in vain.

Wars of religion took on a very disgusting colour and smell on "Belgian soil": red as blood flooding from beheaded martyrs, and sickening as burnt flesh.

The Protestant Reformation had begun in 1517 with Luther's writings in Germany; those writings and ideas were finding good soil and were taking root in "Belgium". This was not at all pleasing to Emperor Charles V or his son Philip II of Spain, who had authority on this territory and who, as Catholic monarchs, were very much in favour of a Counter-Reformation.

Did you know that the first Protestant martyrs were burned alive in Brussels, on 1 July 1523?[1] Brought to Brussels, thrown in jail, interrogated by various inquisitors, and threatened with execution, Hendrik Voes and Johann van Esschen, brothers of the Antwerp Augustinian monastery who had embraced Luther's doctrine, refused to recant. Their inquisitors prepared a document detailing sixty-two articles of heterodox faith which was sufficient evidence to condemn them as heretics. On the Grand Place in Brussels, refusing the offers of last-minute reprieve, Voes and van Esschen were fastened to stakes. Torches brought fire to the wood. According to reports, the two young men sang *Te Deum Laudamus* before succumbing to the smoke and flames.

---

1 See focusonbelgium.be/en/facts/did-you-know-first-protestant-martyrs-were-burned-alive-brussels and "The First Martyrs of Reformation", on lutheranforum.com/blog/the-first-martyrs-of-the-reformation. Thanks to the then-relatively new technology, the printing press, within days, pamphlets detailing the deaths of the two Antwerp brothers were printed and distributed. In one of the pamphlets, the anonymous author clearly sympathises with the victims, painting the authorities as villains and their executions as a gross miscarriage of justice. The tract became a bestseller of sorts: editions were printed by various printers, one as far away as Augsburg.

Following this, Protestants were persecuted by the thousand, in what was called the "Holy Spanish Inquisition" as they refused to renounce their new Reformed faith. Years later, in 1568 on the same Grand Place, the counts of Egmont and Hoorn, who were leading the political opposition to the King of Spain and his imposed Catholicism, were beheaded. Nineteen other noblemen were beheaded in the Grand Sablon square in Brussels.

Butchery. Bloodshed. Again.
This time, in the name of God.

Fires were burning on Belgian soil, and they were not of the right kind. Or, let us put it another way: King Philip of Spain, son of Charles V, Catholic emperor of an "empire on which the sun never sets", had decided to fight fire by fire: whilst the fire of Reformation was burning brightly in Flanders, Brussels and Wallonia, the sinister Duke of Alba, from the Dominican order, was sent to kindle other fires to stop what Spain was perceiving as heresy—and a political threat to its power.

More than 10,000 people were sentenced by the much feared "Rebellion Council". However, in spite of this repression, the Reformation movement continued to spread: in 1566, there were, it seems, 300,000 Protestants in "Belgium", that is to say, 20 percent of the population.[2]

---

2 See museeprotestant.org/en/notice/protestantism-in-belgium/.
  Another fact to illustrate how many "Belgians" were Protestant is that between 1578 and 1585, the major cities had a Calvinistic city council: Brussels, Antwerp, Bruges, Ghent, Charleroi...

But the persecution was harsh. After the death of Philip II, the Archdukes Albert and Isabelle (1598–1633) went on to support the Jesuits in their project of eliminating the Protestants. It was quite efficient. The ones on fire for their new-found faith fled to the North. The ones who stayed re-converted to Catholicism or learned to put their light under a bushel. Quite efficient as, today, the Belgians are still known for their sense of compromise—not burning too hot, moderate. Not a radical middle. Just a middle...[3]

Yet, the fire of Reformation had burned brightly in our regions. Brilliant minds like Tyndale, Erasmus, Plantin Moretus, were present around the same period on "Belgian soil".[4] Three intellectual men who would have a deep influence and impact on the whole of Europe.

William Tyndale[5] was a pivotal figure in the preparation of the first English language Bible translation to be printed. His achievement helped unite the English people. Tyndale worked in Antwerp between 1526 and 1536, having been forced to flee Cologne. He was captured by the troops of Charles V, condemned as a heretic, strangled and burned. In a letter written from prison in Vilvoorde,[6] he asked for warmer

---

3 As the "Holy Spanish Inquisition" battled the fire of Reformation with the fire of literal burnings, many who had embraced the Reformed faith had to retreat. This left the country with a peculiar spiritual atmosphere. When fire cancels fire, you end up... lukewarm?

4 We could also name Willem van Oranje, Marnix van Sint-Aldegonde, Petrus Dathenus.

5 See museumplantinmoretus.be/en.

6 There is a statue of Tyndale on the Grand-Place of Vilvoorde, right in front of a restaurant called *The King of Spain*, which is quite telling. The city still remembers—and the protagonists are there facing one another.

clothes, but especially for his Hebrew Bible. His last words were: "Lord, open the King of England's eyes," and one year later this king allowed an English Bible translation! Vilvoorde, nearby Brussels, was a centre of religious repression towards the faith.[7]

Around the same period, Erasmus lived in Brussels and worked on a new edition of the New Testament. Today, you can still visit "Erasmus' House" in Anderlecht in Brussels. His major work was his translation of the New Testament from Greek into Latin, which replaced the thousand year old Saint Jerome version, known as the Vulgate. Although his work was only written in Latin and Greek, it was translated in his own lifetime into various vernacular languages (English, German, French, Italian, Hungarian and Spanish.)[8]

Last but not least (what would a book be without a printer?), Christophe/Christoffel Plantin was present in Antwerp around the same period. He became the most important printer-publisher of his time. In 1555, he released his first book. Soon after, writers and scientists found their way to his printing office.

---

7 See williamtyndalemuseum.be. Tyndale was burnt in 1536; his last words were: "Lord, open the King of England's eyes," and one year later this king allowed a Bible translation into English!

8 See erasmushouse.museum/en. Erasmus was a kind of "double" figure: on the one hand he studied the Bible very deeply, on the other hand he chose explicitly against Luther and was already a bit "liberal" in his faith. For him, Christianity was more about the moral commandments than about the blood of Jesus.

The quality of his printing was unmatched. In less than twenty years, Plantin's publishing house had become the foremost in Europe. His greatest venture, the Biblia regia, which would establish the original text of the Old and New Testaments in a set of eight volumes was supported by Philip II of Spain, in spite of clerical opposition.

When Antwerp was plundered by the Spaniards in 1576, Plantin established a branch office in Paris and then, in 1583, settled in Leiden as the typographer of the new university of the states of Holland, leaving his much-reduced business in Antwerp in the hands of his son-in-law, John Moretus.

With respect to bloodshed, Belgium was not finished with it following the religious wars of the 16th century, involving the Spanish and the Catholic Inquisition.

More bloody episodes were on their way, with other "empires".

After the Battle of Waterloo and "the birth of a nation", two world wars would happen on the soil of the little "buffer zone".

This time they would be fought against the German empire.

9. Resisting until death: World War I: Ypres

The voice of your brother's blood cries unto Me from the ground.

Genesis 4:10 NIV

Most European battles throughout history are said to have been fought on Belgian territory. In the twentieth century alone, during the two World Wars, Belgium played an important role and paid an enormous price.

World War I is also known as "the Great War" (*la Grande Guerre* in French): "great" because of its length, scope and the fact it was a global war… as well as real "butchery", as many soldiers who were present on the Front described it. It was one of the deadliest conflicts in history.

On 22 April 1915, German attack featured a weapon that had not been used before—namely poison gas. That battle happened in Ypres, a small city in Flanders, in the northern part of Belgium, and marked the Germans' first large-scale use of lethal poison gas as a weapon: "yellow gas", "mustard gas", or "*gaz moutarde*" in French.

Why Ypres—you may ask? The defence of Ypres was key to the British hold on this sector of the Western Front. The town was an important strategic landmark blocking the route for the Imperial German Army through to the French coastal ports.

A British officer watched as one gas cloud approached his position. Here is what he wrote:

> *"Just at dawn they opened a very heavy fire, especially machine-gun fire, and the idea of that was apparently to make you get down. And then the next thing we heard was this sizzling—you know, I mean you could hear this damn stuff coming on—and then saw this awful cloud coming over. A great yellow, greenish-yellow, cloud. It wasn't very high... Nobody knew what to think. But immediately it got there we knew what to think, I mean we knew what it was. Well then of course you immediately began to choke, then word came: whatever you do don't go down. You see if you got to the bottom of the trench you got the full blast of it because it was heavy stuff, it went down."* [1]

What are the effects of mustard gas? It strips away the mucous membranes of the eyes, nose and respiratory tract and, as a consequence, victims may experience irritation of the eyes, temporary blindness, runny nose, cough, shortness of breath and sinus pain. The digestive tract is also affected, resulting in abdominal pain, diarrhea, fever and vomiting. A butchery, the soldiers wrote in their letters from the Front.

Not only was it butchery because of the poison gas, but also because it was a war fought in trenches.

1 iwm.org.uk/history/voices-of-the-first-world-war-gas-attack-at-ypres.

Trenches were like deep wounds in the ground. The soldiers were literally "in the entrails of the earth"—in holes that had been dug deep down. So, when they died, their blood went deep into the ground. Some were even buried alive.

Conditions in the trenches were quite disgusting, with all sorts of pests living there, such as rats, lice, frogs... They made the soldiers itch horribly and caused a disease called 'Trench Fever'. The weather also contributed to rough conditions in the trenches.

Talk about shock and trauma, for the ones who managed to come back alive after such a war; talk about blood crying and soil groaning. Speak of a deep and lasting wound, both in the natural and spiritual world.

From 1914 to 1918, in Flanders Field, one million soldiers from more than fifty different countries were wounded, missing or killed in action.[2] Ypres and Passchendaele became worldwide symbols for the senselessness of war. The peaceful region still bears witness to this history in monuments, museums, cemeteries and the countless individual stories that link it with the world.

Even today, more than a century later, Ypres has not forgotten. The Menin Gate, a memorial arch in the centre of Ypres, has the names of 54,000 missing men engraved on its walls. The Gate is built across the road out of Ypres

2 "Dodengang", "Boyau de la mort", "Trench of Death"—you see them depicted in the *Wonder Woman* movie of 2017. See flandersfields.be/en for more details on the trenches.

that the soldiers would march along, heading towards battle. It was completed in 1927 as a monument. Since 1926, Belgian volunteer firefighters have played the Last Post under the gate every night at 8 p.m. to remember the dead.

Civilians too paid a huge price in this war. *The Rape of Belgium*[3] is the name given to the mistreatment of Belgian civilians by German troops during the invasion and occupation of Belgium during World War I. The neutrality of Belgium had been guaranteed by the Treaty of London (1839). However, the German Schlieffen Plan required that German armed forces pass through Belgium (thus violating Belgium's neutrality) in order to outflank the French Army. At the beginning of the war, the German army engaged in numerous atrocities against the civilian population of Belgium, including the destruction of civilian property.[4]

This "Rape of Belgium" is important as a collective trauma which needs healing. Increasingly, psychologists today are beginning to realise the importance of collective trauma and to write about how to heal it. A recent book called *Healing*

---

3 See Larry Zuckerman, *The Rape of Belgium: The Untold Story of World War I*, New York University Press 2004

4 The Germans were responsible for the deaths of 23,700 Belgian civilians and caused further thousands of permanent or temporary invalids, with 18,296 children becoming war orphans. Around 3,000 Belgian civilians died due to electric fences the German Army put up to prevent civilians from fleeing the country and 120,000 became forced labourers, with half of that number deported to Germany. 25,000 homes and other buildings in 837 communities were destroyed in 1914 alone. 1.5 million Belgians (20% of the entire population) fled from the invading German army.

Collective Trauma: A Process for Integrating Our Intergenerational and Cultural Wounds,[5] explores the symptoms, habits, unconscious social agreements, and cultural shadows that lead to unhealed collective suffering.

It may also be noted that Ypres was one of the sites that hosted an unofficial Christmas Truce in 1914 between German and British soldiers. In addition, during World War II, at the Ypres-Comines Canal, the British Expeditionary Force (BEF) fought the Germans in a delaying action, that helped allow the Allied retreat to Dunkirk.

Small cities in small countries can play an important role at strategic times. Kings of small countries can also distinguish themselves powerfully at such times. Such was Albert I, who was King of the Belgians at this moment in history.

---

5 *Healing Collective Trauma: A Process for Integrating Our Intergenerational and Cultural Wounds* by Thomas Hübl, published by Sounds True Inc, January 2021.

10. *Brave Little Belgium* and King Albert's Book

The King is mighty, He loves justice—You have established equity; in Jacob You have done what is just and right.

Psalm 99:4 NIV

At the start of World War I, King Albert refused to comply with Germany's request for safe passage for its troops through Belgium in order to attack France. The German invasion of Belgium brought Britain into the war as one of the guarantors of Belgian neutrality under the Treaty of 1839.

King Albert, as required by the Belgian constitution, took personal command of the Belgian Army, and held the Germans off long enough for Britain and France to prepare for the Battle of the Marne (6–9 September 1914). For four years Albert held his ground in the small, unoccupied area behind the Yser River, near Ypres, in Flanders Fields. During this period, King Albert fought alongside his troops and shared their dangers, while his wife, Queen Elisabeth, worked as a nurse at the Front.

Already during the war King Albert I was known as the courageous knight-king of "brave little Belgium", who would achieve undying military fame for himself and his army.[1] This is demonstrated by *King Albert's Book:* a most peculiar publication.

The complete title is *King Albert's Book: A Tribute to the Belgian King and People from Representative Men and Women Throughout the World.* It was a gift book produced for sale at Christmas 1914, published by the *Daily Telegraph* as a compendium of tributes in honour of Belgium's courage during the Great War. It brought together princes, statesmen, authors, religious leaders, VIPs and many other dignitaries. Proceeds benefitted the *Daily Telegraph Belgian Fund.*

How had "little Belgium" been brave? By self-sacrifice in flooding its own territory in order to delay the enemy in its march across the land as the German advance was brought to a halt with the flooding of the Yser plain by the deliberate opening of locks by the Belgian Army.

The courage of Belgium and its king during World War I was celebrated by many leaders and published in *King Albert's Book.*

Let us read the very words chosen by THE RIGHT HON. DAVID LLOYD GEORGE to express tribute to Belgium. They are not well-known, but well worth noting:

> *"It has been the privilege of little nations at different periods in the history of the world to render some signal service to civilisation. That duty Belgium has now been called upon to render to European civilisation, and nobly has she answered the call.*

---

1 encyclopedia.1914-1918-online.net/article/albert_i_king_of_the_ belgians.

It is her heroism that has forced Prussian Junkerdom, its character, and its designs, into the light of day. As long as it intrigued against France, Russia, or Britain, it might have continued to take cover under some plausible, diplomatic pretext; but to assail Belgium it had to come into the open, where its arrogance, its brutality, and its aggressiveness became manifest to the world. It was Belgian valour that exposed the sinister character of Prussian militarism, and when that menace is finally overthrown the most honourable share in the triumph will be due to Belgian sacrifice.

This unfortunate country is now overwhelmed by the barbarian flood; but when the sanguinary deluge subsides Belgium will emerge a great and a glorious land which every lover of liberty will honour, and every tyrant henceforth shun."

Other contributors paying tribute to Belgium included the Archbishop of Canterbury, the Aga Khan and Winston Churchill, First Lord of the Admiralty. Novelist Thomas Hardy composed *Sonnet on the Belgian Expatriation*. Musical scores included one from Edward Elgar entitled *Chantons, Belges, Chantons!* [2]

The words used by artists to decribe the landscape and atmosphere in Belgium during and after World War I are worth reading. Better than thousands of history books, the words written by poets help you feel what happened, not just know it in your head by hearsay.

---

2 vrt.be/vrtnws/en/2014/12/16/daily_telegraph_
britainpaystributetopluckybelgium-1-2183507.

From *Belgium Regrets Nothing* in *Selected Poems* of Edith Wharton:[3]

> *Belgium regrets nothing*
> *Not with her ruined silver spires,*
> *Not with her cities shamed and rent,*
> *Perish the imperishable fires*
> *That shape the homestead from the tent.*
> *Wherever men are staunch and free,*
> *There shall she keep her fearless state,*
> *And homeless, to great nations be*
> *The home of all that makes them great.*

An extract from Laurence Binyon, *Ypres:*

> *She was a city of patience; of proud name...*
> *But on a sudden fierce destruction came...*
> *Tigerishly pouncing: thunderbolt and flame...*
> *She rose, dead, into never-dying fame...*

There are also three poems written by the French-speaking Belgian author, Emile Cammaerts, which were put to music by Edward Elgar: Carillon (1914), *Une voix dans le desert* (1915) and *Le drapeau belge* (1917).

In *Carillon*, the text is highly patriotic. The title refers to Belgian bell towers. In *Une voix dans le désert*, there is no patriotic or sentimental fervour, but instead, a hint of the awful, bleak reality of Flanders fields. A desert indeed—man-made. *Le drapeau belge* is a meditation on the colours of the Belgian flag.

---

3 The epigraph for Wartons'contribution, translated as *"Belgium regrets nothing"*, is a quotation from the Belgian Prime Minister Charles Baron de Broqueville.

Let us reproduce some of the words of those texts. As we know, words have power. They can still resonate or echo centuries later. Until other words are uttered, releasing life.

Carillon, "*Chantons, Belges, chantons!*"

> *Sing, Belgians, sing!*
> *Although our wounds may bleed,*
> *Although our voices break,*
> *Louder than the storm, louder than the guns,*
> *Sing of the pride of our defeats*
> *'Neath this bright Autumn sun,*
> *And sing of the joy of honour*
> *When cowardice might be so sweet.*

Une Voix dans le Désert, opening text:

> *A hundred yards from the trenches,*
> *Close to the battle-front,*
> *There stands a little house,*
> *Lonely and desolate.*
> *Not a man, not a bird, not a dog, not a cat,*
> *Only a flight of crows along the railway line,*
> *The sound of our boots on the muddy road*
> *And, along the Yser, the twinkling fires.*

And now, last but not least, the text, *The Belgian Flag*, set to music by Elgar. It was first performed at the birthday concert for King Albert I in the Queen's Hall, London, on 14 April 1917. The original words were in French and an English translation was provided by Lord Curzon of Kedleston.

The Belgian Flag

1. *Red for the blood of soldiers,*
   — Black, yellow and red —
   Black for the tears of mothers,
   — Black, yellow and red —
   And yellow for the light and flame
   Of the fields where the blood is shed!
   . . .

2. *Red for the purple of heroes,*
   — Black, yellow and red —
   Black for the veils of widows,
   Black, yellow and red —
   Yellow for the shining crown
   Of the victors who have bled!
   . . .

3. *Red for the flames in fury,*
   — Black, yellow and red —
   Black for the mourning ashes,
   — Black, yellow and red —
   And yellow of gold, as we proudly hail
   The spirits of the dead!
   To the flag, my sons!
   Your country with her blessing "Forward" cries!
   Has it shrunken? No, when smallest,
   Larger, statelier it flies!
   Is it tattered? No, 'tis stoutest
   When destruction it defies![4]

---

4 For the whole poem, both in its original language, French, and in its
English translation, see wikiwand.com/en/Le_drapeau_belge.

This text *"me prend au ventre,"* as we say in French. My heart of compassion and my travailing as an intercessor are stirred up. Moreover, the colours of the Belgian flag, have been *"seen"* in their spiritual dimension at different times of prayer for Belgium. The words received were the following: when the red of the cross will have covered the black of death, the yellow of glory and grace will cover the land.

From the voice of bells that were courageously ringing, to a territory turned into a desert, where the voice is uttered but no more heard, into a flag and national honour bathed in blood, those texts help us understand and feel what has happened in Belgium.

And pray for further healing and restoration, of health and calling. The courage and self-sacrifice of the nation was manifested, seen and celebrated by many worldwide. Yet the death toll and lasting effect on the people and their territory was enormous. Or, in other words, the expression of the calling and direct retaliation against it, went hand in hand.[5]

---

5 We come back to this in Part Three of this book.

Belgium, Come Forth!

11. Resisting until death: World War II: Bastogne

Whoever sheds the blood of man, by man shall his blood be shed, for God made man in His own image.

Genesis 9:6 ESV

Lest innocent blood be shed in your land that the Lord your God is giving you for an inheritance, and so the guilt of bloodshed be upon you.

Deuteronomy 19:10 ESV

While the northern part of Belgium—Ypres in Flanders—was instrumental in stopping enemy troops in World War I, the southern part of "beautiful Belgium" would valiantly resist and become the turning point in the victory against Nazi Germany at the end of World War II: this happened in Bastogne and the Battle of the Bulge in the Ardennes.

Here again, the conditions of that battle were quite unusual. It was waged in harsh, wintry conditions, around Christmas time—with about 8 inches of snow on the ground and an average temperature of 20 Fahrenheit (about −7°C, with temperatures sometimes −28° Celsius at night!)[1] In the small,

---

1 See for more information europeremembers.com/destination/ bastogne-war-museum.

pivotal[2] Belgian town of Bastogne, the Germans surrounded thousands of Allied troops. The Allied forces had everything going against them; the city was surrounded, they were outnumbered 5 to 1, medical and ammunition supplies were rapidly depleting, and they were in the depths of a winter they were ill-equipped to handle.

Anthony C. McAuliffe was the U.S. Army general who commanded the force defending Bastogne, in the Battle of the Bulge.[3] He was in charge of the entire division when the Germans counterattacked in the Ardennes. On 22 December 1944, the Germans dispatched a small delegation under a flag of truce to deliver an ultimatum. Entering the American lines southeast of Bastogne, the delegation delivered the following message to General McAuliffe, reproduced here to help you view the dire straits in which Bastogne and the troops found themselves:

"To the U.S.A. Commander of the encircled town of Bastogne.

The fortune of war is changing. This time the U.S.A. forces in and near Bastogne have been encircled by strong German armored units…There is only one possibility to save the encircled U.S.A. troops from total annihilation: that is the honorable surrender of the encircled town. In order to think it over a term of two hours will be granted beginning with the presentation of this note.

---

2 Note that this word "pivotal" about Ypres and Bastogne are used by many in relating the strategic battles fought on Belgian soil.

3 As the Germans drove into the Ardennes, the Allied line took on the appearance of a large bulge, giving rise to the battle's name.

If this proposal should be rejected one German Artillery Corps and six heavy A.A. Battalions are ready to annihilate the U.S.A. troops in and near Bastogne. The order for firing will be given immediately after this two hours term.

All the serious civilian losses caused by this artillery fire would not correspond with the well-known American humanity.

The German Commander.

According to those present when McAuliffe received the German message in Bastogne, he read it, crumpled it into a ball, threw it in a wastepaper basket, and muttered, "Aw, nuts." [4] The official reply was typed and delivered to the German delegation. It was as follows:

To the German Commander

NUTS!

The American Commander.

As a result of this answer, the German Luftwaffe attacked the town, bombing it nightly.

Due to bad weather the American forces could not be re-supplied by air, nor was tactical air support available.[5]

---

4 In plainer English, "Go to hell!"

5 For more details, see belgiumremembers44-45.be and history.com/topics/world-war-ii/battle-of-the-bulge.

General Eisenhower, the supreme Allied commander, and Lieutenant-General Patton led the American defence to restore the front. The Christmas gift that Patton desperately wanted was for the weather to clear, so that he could move his armed forces and to allow air support for his operations. He told his chaplain, Colonel James O'Neill, that he was going to demand prayer from him.[6]

Patton had the words of Father O'Neill's prayer set in type in Luxembourg City and distributed a quarter of a million wallet-size cards, with a holiday greeting on the other side.

Prayers rose up and, on that cold Christmas morning, 1944, the weather conditions finally (and quite miraculously) cleared. The ground froze solid, the tanks and air forces could finally manoeuvre, and give assistance to all who were previously blocked off. As finally the sky was clearing, the American planes could drop the supplies and the Allied air force could strike.

The day after Christmas, units of Patton's rapidly approaching Third Army finally arrived, broke through the German lines, and rescued the troops. Less than four months after the end of the Battle of the Bulge, Germany surrendered to Allied forces.

Called "the greatest American battle of the war" by Winston Churchill, the Battle of the Bulge lasted six brutal weeks, from 16 December 1944 to 25 January 1945. The assault took place

---

6 From historynet.com/pattons-last-christmas.htm.

across 85 miles (140 km) of the densely wooded Ardennes Forest. Also called the Battle of the Ardennes, it proved to be the costliest ever fought by the U.S. Army.

The formerly serene, wooded region of the Ardennes was hacked into chaos by fighting as the Americans dug in against the German advance. "Did you ever see land when a tornado's come through? Did you ever see trees and stuff, twisted and broken off? The whole friggin' forest was like that," said U.S. Army soldier Charlie Sanderson.[7]

Sometimes, even the landscape is marked by human violences and "remembers".

---

7 Charley Valera, *My Father's War: Memories from Our Honored WWII Soldiers*, iUniverse 2016

12. Becoming the Heart of Europe

Now the whole world had one language and a common speech... They said to each other... "Come, let us build ourselves a city, with a tower that reaches to the heaven so that we may make a name for ourselves otherwise we will be scattered over the face of the whole earth."

Genesis 11:1–4 NIV

I exhort therefore, that, first of all, supplications, prayers, intercessions, and giving of thanks, be made for all men; for kings, and for all that are in authority; that we may lead a quiet and peaceable life in all godliness and honesty.

1 Timothy 2:1–2 KJV

In 1951, six years after the end of World War II, the leaders of six European countries (Belgium, Luxembourg, The Netherlands, France, Italy and West Germany) signed the Treaty of Paris which created the European Coal and Steel Community (ECSC). The idea was that by asking France and Germany to unite around their coal and steel supplies, the material resources for war would be under check.

With this new community came the first European institutions. A number of cities were considered, and Brussels would have been accepted as a compromise, but the Belgian government put all its effort into backing Liège, opposed by all the other members, and was unable to formally back Brussels due to internal instability.[1]

Agreement remained elusive and a seat had to be found before the institutions could begin work, hence Luxembourg was chosen as a provisional seat, though with the Common Assembly in Strasbourg as that was the only city with a large enough hemicycle.[2] This agreement was temporary.

The 1957 Treaties of Rome established two new communities, the European Economic Community (EEC) and the European Atomic Energy Community (Euratom). Discussions on the seats of the institutions were left till the last moment before the treaties came into force, so as not to interfere with ratification. Brussels waited until only a month before talks to enter its application, despite widespread support. The Belgian government eventually pushed its campaign and started large-scale construction for use by the institutions.

A Committee of Experts deemed Brussels to be the one option to have all the necessary features for a European capital:

---

1 Thierry Demey, *Brussels, capital of Europe*. S. Strange (trans.). Brussels: Badeaux, 2007

2 A hemicycle is a horseshoe shape structure for legislative assemblies such as the one used by the Council of Europe.

- a large, active metropolis, without a congested centre or poor quality of housing;
- good communications with other member states' capitals, including to major commercial and maritime markets;
- vast internal transport links; an important international business centre;
- plentiful housing for European civil servants; and an open economy.

Furthermore, it was located on the border between the two major European civilisations, Latin and Germanic, and was at the centre of the first post-war integration experiment: the Benelux. As the capital of a small country, it also could not claim to use the presence of the institutions to exert pressure on other Member States, it being more of a neutral territory between the major European powers. The committee's report was approved.[3]

Today, the European Commission and the European Council are located in Brussels. Although the formal seat of the European Parliament is still in Strasbourg, where voting takes place, formal meetings of political groups and committee groups take place in Brussels and three quarters of Parliamentary sessions now take place at its Brussels hemicycle.[4]

Brussels is greatly considered internationally as the capital of the European Union. That is why many national television

---

3 Extract from Thierry Demey, *Brussels, capital of Europe* (S. Strange trans.), Ed. Badeaux 2007; available from wikipedia.
4 There are an estimated 25,000 lobbyists working in Brussels.

stations, as they debrief the decisions taken by the Union end up saying, "Brussels has decided"—meaning by this that the EU has taken that decision.

Is it such a surprise that this city which, through the centuries, has hosted the seat of government of the Spanish, the Austrians, the French and the Dutch; is located in a buffer state created to balance powers in Europe; where the Germans, British and Americans gathered during World War I and II and fought "pivotal battles"; where the Germanic and Roman worlds and languages meet (or collide)—would have finally been chosen to become the capital city of a European Union?[5]

We could say that the city/country fulfils the function it had been created for. Belgium and Brussels continue to function as a buffer zone, where wars should be prevented. Only, today the wars have shifted from political to economic ones. Today, in Brussels, the nations gather to discuss quotas, fish or milk quotas, free-market and possible obstacles to trade...

---

5 About the "living together" of different langages and cultures on "Belgian ground", see the book *Zinc* by David van Reybrouck. The book is set in Neutral Moresnet, a completely forgotten mini-state that is now part of German-speaking Belgium but from 1816 to 1919 had its own flag, its own government and even its own national anthem (in Esperanto). Neutral Moresnet was a small Belgian-Prussian condominium administered jointly by the United Kingdom of the Netherlands (Belgium after its independence in 1830) and the Kingdom of Prussia. It was 1 mile (1.6 km) wide and 3 miles (4.8 km) long, with an area of 900 acres (360 ha). Moresnet reminds us that German is the third official language of Belgium, spoken by a small community in the south-east of the country.

The battles can be fierce (think about the ones over fisheries or, more recently, over the conditions for Brexit), yet, till now, bloodshed has been prevented—at least, in the natural.

The pressures in this city can be huge, especially when Europe enters a crisis and extra Summits of Heads of States and Governments need to be hosted, with security measures that end up blocking the traffic in the city centre and its tunnels.

If Europe is in pain, Brussels often suffers.

Brussels is where lobbies and embassies are extra-numerous (you duplicate the Ambassadors to Belgium with Ambassadors to the European Union).

It's where, so many say, you find the best interpreters and diplomats of the world.

It's where the statue of Europa on her bull has long been exhibited in front of the European Council Building and the references to the gods of Greece are omnipresent in the decoration, pieces of art and even the document management systems used by the civil servants (Arès, Hermès and so on).

It's where the name given to the European Parliamant's building is *Le Caprice des dieux*, because of its shape.[6]

---

6 Oval, like the shape of the box of the French camembert called "caprice des dieux".

And because names often tend to manifest the nature of things and beings, it's where Babel was the name given to one of the first assistance programmes for the translation of documents used by the European Commission.

It's also where the 27 flags of the 27 European nations that once proudly flew in the wind in front of the Commission Building have been replaced by 27 starry banners of Europe. (This, despite the motto used by Jean Monnet, one of the founding fathers of the European Community, "Nous ne coalisons pas des Etats, nous unissons des peuples"—*We are not forming coalitions of states, we are uniting men.*)

Brussels has become the seat of the European institutions. Or, as some say, "the heart of Europe". Fulfilling her calling to act as a "buffer zone", balancing powers and guaranteeing peace to the surrounding nations.

Yet Europe needs prayer in order not to lose her heart or lose heart. Europe needs our prayers, your prayers.

Are we not all called to make supplications, intercessions for our governing authorities?

Are not the European institutions governing you and your life if you are French, Dutch, Spanish, Italian, Finnish, Greek and so many other? Are they not having an influence on your economies if you are American, Australian, British?

Pray, make supplications on her behalf.

Without prayer, Europe is in danger of becoming a *world of one language and common speech, a city built by and for ourselves, with bricks in place of stones, a tower that reaches to the heaven—but without God.*

Don't leave the burden of intercession for Europe on the shoulders of Brussels only. After all, there are twenty-six countries and more than 450 million people. The yoke is not easy, the burden is not light.[7] Yet much is at stake.

It is about two models, two blueprints: a coalition of States—or an empire.

---

7 Comparing the European Union's new facility in Strasbourg with the medieval painter Brueghel's *Tower of Babel* has occurred to not a few, Christians and non-Christians alike. See for more details on the buildings of the EU: architectureehereandthere.com/2016/12/28/eu-new-brussels-hq.

13. Heart seizures and heart attacks

For the enemy has pursued my soul, he has crushed my life to the ground, he has made me sit in darkness like those long dead. Therefore my spirit faints within me; my heart within me is appalled.

Psalm 143:3–4 ESV

I would have lost heart, unless I had believed that I would see the goodness of the Lord in the land of the living.

Psalm 27:13 NKJV

Do you know that the centre of Brussels, the "Pentagon" as it is called, has the shape of a heart?

Do you know that when Europe is in crisis, the arteries of the city are blocked and the heart of Brussels is stopped in a traffic jam?

Brussels is given the blame so often (cursed?) when any decisions taken are not pleasing to one country or another. This city is confronted by the anger of those who feel unfairly treated. Many demonstrations are held in front of the European Institutions, again often blocking access to the heart of the city. There is not often joy or thankfulness for the benefits received.

121

In recent years, Brussels has been regularly ranked as one of the most congested cities in western Europe. This is due to Belgium's high population density and large number of commuters as well as these social and political demonstrations. Consider the ones about climate change, with thousands of young people marching through the streets before stopping in front of the European Institutions.

The good news is that, as the heart of Europe, Brussels is a governmental city where the voice of the people can be heard. But the concert of voices can sometimes be overbearing and chaotic. In 2018, the city of Brussels registered 995 demonstrations (!), its highest score ever. And 80% of those demonstrations had nothing to do with Belgium.

As if the heart of Brussels was pumping more for Europe than for Belgium, as if the weight carried and blood pressure experienced as capital of the EU was far higher than the one to function as capital of the nation as such.

Pray for your European authorities, pray for Brussels, as much is decided in that city that goes far beyond her small territory.

You don't want the heart of Europe to fail, you don't want it to break.[1]

---

1 Interesting to note: there is a sickness called "broken-heart syndrome" or "Takotsubo cardiomyopathy", named after *an octopus trap*. It is a weakening of the left ventricle, the heart's main pumping chamber, usually as the result of severe emotional or physical stress. Think of all the heart-breaking conflicts described in Part II of this book, and of a heart that needs to "pump blood" for Europe.

I know this is a vivid metaphor, yet I use it on purpose. In different meetings over the last years, prophetic intercessors gathered in Brussels have heard the heartbeat of the city.

One day, intercessors heard the beautiful and intense beats of that strong heart, pumping and distributing blood into the whole country and into the rest of Europe. Another day, while gathered in the Brussels House of Prayer, close to the European Institutions, with intercessors from different parts of the country, the heart that we saw was so much under attack that it had almost stopped beating. We had to prophesy life back to it, almost to give it a cardiac massage through prayer. Knowing that if it would stop beating, the whole of Europe would be affected.

Strike at the heart! We know this expression and strategic advice, often used in wartime.

Remember what was said about Belgium in World War I and World War II: small but pivotal. If you can make it there, you can make it everywhere. If you can win there, you can win everywhere.

The holy patron of the city of Brussels reminds us of this: his name is Michaël, Sint-Michaël—the warring archangel who fought against the fallen angels and against the one leading their rebellion. You can still see him (as a statue) striking the dragon on the top of the tower of the City Hall in the Grand Place!

As the movement "Resurrection Belgium" puts it, "Battles won in Belgium are battles won for Europe." The man carrying that vision[2] even shares that those words, "Strike the enemy at the heart," were given to him while in prayer in America for Europe, before he knew that Brussels was called "the heart of Europe".

Strike at the heart!

God's children know the strategy – and the enemy too.

Protect the heart. Pray for Brussels.

The winner in Brussels takes it all in Europe.

Make sure the kingdom of Light prevails in that city.

You don't want "the Empire to strike back" in that strategic place.

Make sure that the heart of the project is preserved, the good and godly mandate fulfilled. Make sure the heart keeps beating and pumping Blood to the whole European body.

---

2 Matthew King, *Resurrection Belgium,* facebook.com/
 resurrectionbelgiummovement/.

The Answer

14. Reopening the books, remembering

The court was convened, and the books were opened.

Daniel 7:10 NASB

On that night the king could not sleep; and he commanded to bring the book of records of the chronicles, and they were read before the king.

Esther 6:10 KJV

Part of healing from trauma, which has fragmented a person or a territory, is remembering.

Re-membering, bringing back together.

Putting a stop to what dis-mantles, what removes the mantle of honor, leaving the creature naked, ashamed, wounded, in shock and isolation.

Remember, remember, Belgium! Don't forget.

Re-member, re-member Belgium.

For this, you have to look at what happened.

The ten chapters of the second part of this book tried to help do that. Belgium, your wounds went deep. And the wounds you inflicted on others (your colonies) went very deep too. Don't try to attend to this hurt lightly.

Don't let others tell you it was a small matter, that you should be over it by now. Have there not been enough conferences and prayers already, enough words of forgiveness uttered? Enough well-meaning prophecies of a bright future given? Enough encouragement given to now stand up and arise?

Well, let us consider. Was Lazarus able to arise and shine, after he was resurrected? Was there not a command given by Jesus to the ones standing around? An unwrapping required, which Lazarus could not have performed all by himself? A re-membering of what had disintegrated and had begun to stink.

What was Lazarus' smell after his resurrection? Was he "on the nose"? Did his friends want to approach and help unwrap him? Those garments of death, they can take some time and care to be removed. And resurrection can be a risky business. Don't we read that, after his resurrection, Lazarus' life was in danger as the sign he had become was not pleasing to the religious elite of the day?

A measure of healing has already taken place in Belgium, and we are grateful for it. Yet, it has not gone deep enough.[1] It

---

1 Let us say here that, in this present season, the French-speaking
  intercessors of Belgium feel this more acutely than the Flemish ones.

was not a small thing what happened to this land, and it is no good saying, "All is well now." The prophet Jeremiah reminds us of that risk:

> *"For they have healed the hurt of the daughter of My people slightly, saying, Peace, peace; when there is no peace."*

Jeremiah 8:11 KJV

Let us not be like that. Let us not be like Job's friends either, who came with well-meaning intentions, but wrong advice. In this *Kairos* season, if we want to go higher, we need to go deeper and dare touch painful things that God had allowed to stay untouched till now because they are terribly painful.[2]

Also, Brussels, remember your calling.

Open your history books and remember that from long ago, you were called to become a capital city, both to what would become Belgium and what would become Europe.

Remember how it all began, in this little neighbourhood of Saint-Géry, by the Senne, by the water.

---

2 Belgium is like a person (as pointed out in the appendix): if you have been traumatised, you tend to bury the memories alive and/or remember only parts of what happened. The only total truth about a person/ country is recorded in heaven; that is why we need to reopen the book in heaven. As with king Ahasuerus, God kept him awake during that *kairos* night, in order to have some forgotten truths revealed. In this season, who should be kept awake to listen in Belgium? the king? the prophet? the intercessor?...

Remember the good parts of your history, with Géry, his joy, his faith, his healing balm.

Remember your Golden Age as "Burgundy", when you had different boundaries and you were flourishing, defying an empire. Remember your spiritual inheritance, your Flemish Mystics, who were trilingual: who spoke Latin, French and Dutch with the same ability and pleasure, sharing their revelations and wisdom with the rest of Europe.

Remember your Reformation time: the courage of your martyrs: your anointing to translate the Book: to print and spread the Good News.

Remember your Knight-King and King Albert's book, a tribute to your bravery.

Remember. Join the dots.

As you remember, connections and re-connections are being made. Your belt of truth is being restored.[3] Your body parts begin to come together, like the dry bones in Ezekiel's vision.

Remember, Belgium! Your book is being opened.

---

3 Aletheia is the Greek word for *truth* and comes from "not forgetting". So remembering has to do with truth, as opposed to an agenda to dis-member memory. Dis-mantling, dis-membering: in English, even the root of the words speak of this truth. Literally, alethetia means *un-covering*, or *disclosure of truth*.

15. Exposing the enemy: Leviathan

In that day the Lord will take His terrible, swift sword and punish Leviathan, the swiftly moving serpent, the coiling, writhing serpent. He will kill the dragon of the sea.

Isaiah 27:1 NLT

Awake, awake, put on strength, O arm of the Lord. Wake up as in days past, as in generations of old. Was it not You who cut Rahab to pieces, who pierced through the dragon?

Isaiah 51:9 BSB

Leviathan, the dragon of the sea. What is its relevance here? What has Leviathan to do with all the wars that have stained the ground of Belgium?

Much: if we know that blood is crying from the earth for vindication and if we know that Leviathan is a spiritual entity that retaliates, lashes back.

Much: if we know that this spirit is all about honour and dishonour.

131

As we have seen, many dishonouring acts have happened on Belgian soil: bodies beheaded and burned on the Grand Place of Brussels; young men killed by the thousands and robbed of their teeth in Waterloo; bodies attacked by yellow gas and buried in the depth of the trenches in World War I; rape of civilians in World War II; wealth built by the amputation of hands and feet in Congo… many things that would desecrate a place and a people. Not just once, but repeatedly, almost as a curse, throughout history.

But how does this all concern Leviathan? And, first of all, *what is* Leviathan?

I am not the kind of person who has a lot of spiritual dreams and sees all sorts of spiritual things during the night—this, despite of the fact that I have completed a number of dream schools and have interpreted for prophets who have lots of such dreams. I have what I would call "my three/four spiritual dreams of the year."

So, when during one of those dreams last year (February 2020), I saw that marine creature appear, with very ugly intentions—a dream that left me physically sick the following day and weak for the rest of the week, so ill that I had to call in sick for work, which I very rarely do, I realised that God wanted to draw my attention to this spirit. And I knew it was a "big one" (I thought of it as a *principality*) by the lasting effect this encounter had on me, even if it only happened in a dream.

Also, another person—a Flemish brother—in the prophetic team I was praying with a few months before that night, had also received a dream/picture that he drew for us, about the Leviathan and the sword.

Finally, around the same time in June 2020, the book by Anne Hamilton, *Dealing with Leviathan*, was released.[1] So, I knew the chance was small that all this appearance of Leviathan would just be "random" and that I had to give some attention to that *"coiling serpent"* described in Isaiah 27.

As a coiling serpent, Leviathan **twists communication** and distorts the meaning of words. Consider what that strategy could be when people of two different language groups and cultures try to gather, understand each other and plan action, especially for the Kingdom of Light![2]

Leviathan is described in the books of Psalms, Isaiah, and Job as a water-being (it "frolics in the deep" in Psalm 104:26) with multiple heads and scales, a being that is linked to pride. In her book *Defeating Water Spirits*, Jennifer LeClaire writes that it is no ordinary spirit but a *principality* in the occult hierarchy of hell that rules nations. It is the ultimate gatekeeper of hostility.[3]

---

1 Anne Hamilton, *Dealing with Leviathan: Spirit of Retaliation: Strategies for the Threshold #5*, June 2020, Armour Books. Most of this chapter quotes or is inspired by the revelations shared in that book.

2 Franz Lippi, founder of B.L.A.S.T.—ministries (Graz, Austria), a network of international intercession and church planting in South-East Europe (Balkan — see www.blastministries.net) defines Leviathan as the spirit of division. Indeed, mis-communication often leads to division.

3 Jennifer LeClaire, *The Spiritual Warriors' Guide to Defeating Water Spirits. Overcoming Demons that Twist, Suffocate, and Attack God's Purposes for Your Life*, 2018, Destiny Image Publishers.

This aspect of gatekeeper is interesting, as it appears also as very central in the description of Leviathan's function given by Anne Hamilton: a *threshold guardian*.

A threshold is a boundary in space or time or physical state.[4] About *time*, Jennifer LeClaire indicates *that there is a Kairos time for a Leviathan spirit against your life. Crocodiles attack during breeding seasons. So beware of Leviathan in periods of spiritual growth or spiritual birthing. All those seasons are prime times for pride in your heart to open the door to Leviathan.*

Dragons **attack at a time of crossing over or giving birth**. *They want you to run from God's transitions and new births in your life—to abort or abandon what He has called you to be or do.*

This is important to know about and be aware of.

Anne Hamilton describes how Leviathan manifests, in that *we sense its presence when we describe our* **situation as involving retribution, payback, backlash, blowback, kickback, whiplash, repercussions, reprisal or revenge**. *Its symbol is the crocodile, scorpion or anything with lashing tail, such as a stingray. It may also be imagined as a dragon, whale,[5] hydra, manticore or basilik. Actions indicating his presence are flame-throwing, acid-flicking, incense-burning or a "death-roll"...*

---

4 By "state", this means physical state such as solid/liquid and the temperature boundary between them—for example, between ice and water or water and steam.

5 This is how it manifested in my dream, a mixture of a whale and a shark or nard.

She also points that it is a *"'nachash', that is, a fire-serpent, like the six-winged seraph... The function of the priestly Levites in the Inner Court of the Tabernacle and Temple mirrors the original purpose of Leviathan within the heavenly courts—before its fall. Because the offices of God are irrevocable then, even as a fallen seraph, Leviathan is able to discharge its duty to* **ensure the court is a place of honour and holiness. It is savage in its reprisal against dishonour**... *Its description corresponds to the furniture of the Inner Court: seven heads like the seven-branched menorah; food like the Bread of the Presence; fire and smoke like the incense altar."* [6]

Waow!

Selah.

Pause and think twice.

Prayerfully consider.

If we begin to joint the dots and tick our boxes, something interesting begins to emerge here.

Consider the dragon-marine spirit and the history and legend around the creation of Brussels: born on a water course, the Senne; with as "official saint and patron", Michaël (Saint-Michel in French), on display at the pinnacle of the Hotel de Ville in the Grand Place "defeating the dragon". Consider also the legends and statues of dragons being defeated in other cities of Belgium built on a river: Namur in Wallonia, Antwerp in Flanders.

---

6 This is a direct quote from the book on Leviathan by Anne Hamilton, in Appendix 1, page 213.

Consider Leviathan as a spirit concerned with honour and dishonour, whose coils are powered by dishonour—and think of all the dishonour which has taken place in Belgium, from "the Waterloo teeth", to "the rape of Belgium" in World War I, to the quasi-extermination of Bastogne in World War II; then consider "Leopold's hands and feet" in the Congo and the dishonouring of others. Backlashes. Dishonour piling up on top of other dishonouring deeds.[7]

Dishonouring others creates holes in the Armour of God (Ephesians 6)—whilst at the same time, it empowers the coils of Leviathan. Shields up for him, shields down for us, we could say. Think of Leviathan as the king of the sons of pride; and think of Belgium receiving as its king a possible Grand Master, a Builder-King "lording it" over a colony he has made his own.

Think that pride goes before a fall, and humbling before answered prayer.

Think of how humility is essential to honour, and pride is detrimental to it.

Think of the spiritual atmosphere in Belgium, when one linguistic community refuses to consider the interests of the

---

7 In her book, *Dealing with Resheph, Spirit of Trouble,* Anne Hamilton also states that Leviathan has another "face" or "name" in Scripture: Resheph. This spirit of killing heat—fever, fire, financial chaos, drought, mental and emotional turmoil—is able to trouble us because we have dishonoured God, particularly during prayer. Resheph is also a counterfeit of Jesus as the Chief Cornerstone.

other and bow in order to find a solution that would honour the interests of both.[8]

Think that, even if resurrected, we cannot unwrap ourselves, we need others, as was the case with Lazarus. And how pride keeps us wrapped up, complicit with Leviathan.[9] Also, think that one of the most significant hindrances to answered prayer is pride and dishonour. If you are not getting answers, look to dishonour (given or received) as a possible reason.

Honour, justice, restitution, reconciliation.

Dishonour, unrighteousness, robbery, unforgiveness and division.

One line or the other.

Note also that Leviathan can be both a creature or a blueprint, a system—or, better said, a spirit behind a system. Hobbes, the English philosopher and writer of the 18th century, whose major work is the book *"Leviathan"*, presents it as a system, a necessary monster joining the people of a nation in a social contract. As such, his proposed "Leviathan" is a counterfeit of the Body of Christ, the priestly assembly foreshadowed in the Old Testament by the Levites.

---

8 This can of course go both directions, from French-speaking to Dutch-speaking people and the other way round. And this is only part of the linguistic challenge, as German is the third official language of Belgium, and English is very often used in Brussels and in Christian (inter)national meetings as "common ground". Imagine the possible misunderstandings when people do no speak with the same mother tongue.

9 This consideration is also from Anne Hamilton.

Leviathan's attribute is that of "joining" people or things together much as the Levites "joined" together the tribal confederation through shared worship of Yahweh as they performed their priestly duties. In her book, Anne Hamilton further develops this parallelism. She also states that Leviathan wants our inheritance—symbolised by land and a fruitful vineyard. He wants our birthright. He wants to mark his ownership of our "land" by putting his name on it (he is after the seed, as we see with the dragon in the book of Revelation). Leviathan is empowered to keep us back from our destiny because of unrepented dishonour.

We also know that God's throne (governmental authority) is built on righteousness and justice.[10] And that God answers prayer on behalf of the land when honour has been restored:

> *If My people who are called by My name, will humble themselves, and pray and seek My face, and turn from their wicked ways, then I will hear from heaven, and will forgive their sin and heal their land.*

> 2 Chronicles 7:14 NIV

Where freemasonry is, there is Leviathan—this is one of the observations of Anne Hamilton. On the reverse side, peace/shalom is lethal to Leviathan. Do we begin to see the possible link between Belgium and the frolicking of Leviathan on this territory?

---

10 About unrighteousness and dishonour, think of the Detroux-case mentioned in the foreword of this book: how shameful it is and how deeply desecrating. Consider too that the Palace of Justice of Brussels, a monstrous masonic building erected during the reign of King Leopold II, has been under construction and scaffolding for decades and is known both in Belgium and elsewhere as "the palace of injustice".

16. Finding the true identity

That is why the Levites have no share of property or possession of land among the other Israelite tribes. The Lord Himself is their special possession.

Deuteronomy 10:9 NLT

Then he showed me Joshua the high priest standing before the angel of the Lord, and Satan standing at his right hand to accuse him. And the Lord said to Satan, "The Lord rebuke you, O Satan! The Lord who has chosen Jerusalem rebuke you! Is this not a brand plucked from the fire?" Now Joshua was standing before the angel, clothed in filthy garments. And the angel said to those who were standing before him, "Remove the filthy garments from him." And to him he said, "Behold, I have taken your iniquity away from you, and I will clothe you with pure vestments." And I said, "Let them put a clean turban on his head." ...

And the angel of the Lord solemnly assured Joshua, saying, "Thus says the Lord of hosts: If you will walk in My ways and keep My charge, then you shall rule My house and have charge of My courts, and I will give you the right of access among those who are standing here."

Zechariah 3:1–7 ESV

Selah.
Pause.

Prayerfully consider:

- when we think about Belgium, how it was born, how the duchy or empire it was part of has increased, decreased, changed boundaries through the centuries;
- when we think of the title of its king, King of the Belgians (a people), not King of Belgium (a territory)— as opposed to Queen Elizabeth of England for example;
- when we think that it was created as a buffer zone for Europe, for the benefit and peace of others, to balance powers between the other entities, and placed between them;
- when we remember that Belgium offered itself as a sacrifice during World War I and World War II, flooding its own territory to stop the enemy in Flanders fields, resisting unto death in Bastogne;[1] that it is the place— Brussels—where the first European martyrs of the Protestant Reformation fell;[2]
- when we know that the tribe of Levi—the Levites— was put at the centre of the people of Israel when they were in the camp in the desert after leaving Egypt; that the Levites received no property or possession of land

---

[1] For more information on the price paid by civilians during this war, see bel-memorial.org/books/the-unknown-dead-civilians-in-the-battle-of-the-bulge.pdf.

[2] Where Belgium offers her own brilliant politicians to serve Europe, placing herself in a crisis situation that makes those same nations she has just rescued, laugh: think of the time—more than 365 days—when Belgium was devoid of a federal Government after nominating Herman Van Rompuy as President of the European Council to help Europe have suitable governance, while at the same time Belgium lost her own bilingual Prime Minister, the only man at that time who was acceptable to lead the country and its two linguistic communities, which often diverged in their votes and preferences.

of its own as it was to fulfil the service of the temple, presenting offering for all the other tribes;

— when we know that the Levites served as teachers and judges, maintaining cities of refuge—buffer zones—in Biblical times;

— when we discover that the word "Levi" etymologically means *joined, to be fastened to, devoted to, attached to,* functioning as "glue" or, rather, ligaments, to keep the other tribes united as one body, not dis-membered;

— when we see all that and take it into account, are we not beginning to realise a parallelism between the functioning of Levi towards the other tribes of Israel and the functioning of Belgium towards the other countries of Europe?[3]

Are we not beginning to perceive Leviathan's functioning as a counterfeit to Levi,[4] opposing his efforts to join and unite, in repetitive attempts to divide and fragment?

L'union fait la force is Belgium's national motto. *Unity is strength.*

And, on the contrary, division or fragmentation is weakness.[5]

---

3 A king that is not territorial is very unusual. "King of the Belgians" sounds like the king of a tribe. Levites are a tribe, a priestly tribe. Levites are specifically needed where unity is not (enough) there.

4 Levi/ Leviathan: two names with the same root, pointing to the priesthood and its counterfeit. In the intercessory movement in France (*Houses of Prayer*), they refer more today to "the priesthood according to Melchizedek/Jesus" than according to Levi (Old Testament tribe) but they also expose "the other priesthood" (the counterfeit) that needs to be opposed, through intercession and high praises. For more information on this, see melkisedek.fr.

5 Remember here the revelation shared by Anne Griffith that a nationalistic spirit would tend to rise up on a tectonic plate (in Belgium, the line of separation between the Roman and Germanic worlds) when no (deep enough) healing of the heart has taken place.

When we go deeper into the past of present day Belgium and remember the history/legend around the birth of Brussels, the release of captives and the killing of a dragon by Géry of Cambrai; when we take into account that today Brussels is the city where the European nations gather, the heart of Europe that *"if you make it there (as a hero or as a dragon), you make it everywhere,"* we understand once more the importance of this capital city and the country it is part of. A capital city of prime importance, a strategic place on the end-times chess board.

Pivotal, although small.

"I know two cities where the nations gather, one is Jerusalem, the other one is... Brussels." Those are the words that, to my great amazement, I heard while preparing my first trip to Israel and praying: "Is there anything you want me to be aware of before visiting Israel, Lord?"

The words had been almost audible in my spirit, but they did not seem to make complete sense to my mind, as I directly thought of other cities where nations gather: Geneva, New York…

Yet those words remained with me and I began to meditate further upon what Brussels and Jerusalem could have in common. And elements came.

– In both cities, there is a wall of separation and a deep challenge to co-host two different people, cultures and religions.
– In Jerusalem, the nations in Jesus' time gathered for the feast of Pentecost—and people of all tribes and tongues

will gather there again at the end of time, according to
the book of Revelation.

— In Brussels, 27 nations gather, under one flag, trying to
join together, keep peace, overcome the babelic confusion
of languages[6]—but at risk of building a tower that would
reach to heaven without God.

The parallels—and differences—between the two cities was
beginning to take shape in my mind, yet I would not have
dared to share this idea further nor write about it—until I
happened upon an article written by one of the brightest
minds of Belgium,[7] who is not a professing Christian, but
who wrote the following around the same period that I was
meditating on this matter:

> *Bruxelles, en effet, c'est un peu notre Jérusalem… Bruxelles est une
> ville-symbole à laquelle chacune de nos ethnies prétend avoir un droit
> sacré: les Flamands parce qu'elle est au cœur de leur région et que
> c'est leur langue que le petit peuple de Bruxelles a parlée pendant
> des siècles, les Wallons parce que c'est en français que Bruxelles est
> devenue capitale et que c'est par suite le français qui est aujourd'hui
> la langue la mieux connue des Bruxellois. Lâcher Bruxelles serait de
> ce fait, de part et d'autre, une insupportable humiliation.*

---

6 In the EU institutions, they translate from 24 languages into 24
languages, which leads to 576 possible combinations of languages.

7 Philippe Van Parijs, who directs the Hoover Chair of Economic
and Social Ethics at the University of Louvain and holds a Visiting
Professorship at the Law Faculty of the University of Oxford.

Translated into English, it reads:

> *Brussels, in fact, is a bit like our Jerusalem... Brussels is a city-symbol each of our ethnic groups claims as a sacred right: the Flemish because it is at the heart of their region and because it is their language that the small people of Brussels have spoken for centuries, the Walloons because it is in French that Brussels has become capital and that it is consequently French which is today the best-known language of the inhabitants of Brussels. To let go of Brussels would therefore be an unbearable humiliation on both sides.*

He also speaks of the wall of Jerusalem, the wailing wall, and the "wall" of separation in Brussels, located on Flemish ground, but where a great majority of citizens speak French, separating French- and Dutch-speaking Belgians. We also know that, historically, it separates the Germanic nations from the Roman ones.

Here, if we think of honour and of how Leviathan preys on any form of dishonour, what a challenge there is for this country, where innocent blood, rape, bowing to the false gods of Egypt[8] has been prevalent and, to a certain degree, still permeates the atmosphere. How can we *join, connect, remember* in a godly manner?

---

8 Think of the masonic temple of Amon-Râ located in Brussels; think of the Palace of Justice in Brussels (wmf.org/project/brussels-palace-justice), a colossal construction portrayed in the last album by François Schuiten, *Le Dernier Pharaon/ the Last Pharaoh* (altaplana.be/en/albums/le-dernier-pharaon).

Not in a counterfeit way, like that of joining tiles as the "tiler" of the masonic craft did.[9] Rather, instead, in a priestly way, as the High Priest carrying the breastplate of righteousness did.[10]

What a challenge for a city like Brussels to "bridge the gap", "stand on the wall", take great care in not despising, nor speaking ill of the other communities and linguistic groups, to treat with respect the "foreigners" of the 26 other countries[11] and tongues hosted in the city: and, for those guests to do the same and honour the country that is welcoming them. To leave prejudices behind and "consider the other as superior to myself."

Standing on the wall, to be a bridge builder in a holy way.

Once, whilst praying in Geneva with messianic Jews for the 500th anniversary of the Protestant Reformation in a place close to the *Wall of the Reformers*, I perceived a spiritual connection between those three walls: the one in Jerusalem, the one in Geneva, and the one (the old Roman "limes") in Brussels. It was as if the prayers made at the feet of one wall were directly producing effects on the other ones.

---

9 The "tiler" of freemasonry is, like Leviathan, a threshold guardian. The "tiler" is charged with guarding the door, armed with a sword, to protect the premises.

10 The purpose of the priestly breastplate was to carry the gemstones upon which the names of the twelve tribes of Israel were engraved so they could be brought before God "as a continual memorial". See Exodus 28:17–20. The stones were different one from another. Different stones and different colors, but all placed together in unity.

11 This number, of course, does not include the embassies of non-European countries.

And if the wailing wall of Jerusalem was the model—where prayers are expressed the "oriental way" (and, remember, Jesus was a Jew, not a Greek), with deep emotions, tears, groaning, travailing even—why in Brussels, on this other dividing "wall"/linguistic border, where much has to be bridged and repented of, should we stick to a "stoic way" of petitioning, as if the heart were not involved in the process?

What if, in Brussels, praying at the wall, wailing at the wall, with a heart of compassion and deep travailing in the spirit, could make a difference not only for Belgium, but somehow for Israel and the Middle East?

What if contending in the spirit in that place, on that fault line, could heal the breaches of dishonour and re-member nations?[12]

Selah.
Pause.

Think twice and prayerfully consider...

---

12 Brussels is the second most international city (after Dubai): 184 nationalities! Chuck Pierce, present in Brussels in April 2016, prophesied that Brussels should be a city where the nations join in building an altar of worship. We know that (prophetic) intercession and worship are closely linked.

17. Prophesying life to dry bones: *Belgium, Come Forth!*

> *Then Jesus, again groaning in Himself, came to the tomb. It was a cave, and a stone lay against it. Jesus said, "Take away the stone." Martha, the sister of him who was dead, said to Him, "Lord, by this time there is a stench, for he has been dead four days." Jesus said to her, "Did I not say to you that if you would believe you would see the glory of God?" ... And Jesus lifted up His eyes and... He cried with a loud voice, "Lazarus, come forth!" And he who had died came out...*

John 11:38–44 NKJV

The Belgian national anthem, in its present version, dates from 1860. It is called *La Brabançonne* and its first paragraph has some "prophetic" undertones:

Après des siècles d'esclavage,
Le Belge sortant du tombeau,
A reconquis par son courage,
Son nom, ses droits et son drapeau.
Et ta main souveraine et fière,
Désormais peuple indompté,
Grava sur ta vieille bannière :
Le Roi, la Loi, la Liberté !

Translated into English, it would read like this:

After centuries of slavery,
The Belgian coming out of the tomb,
Has reconquered by his courage,
His name, his rights and his flag.
And your sovereign and proud hand,
Now untamed people,
Engraved on your old banner:
For King, for Law, for Liberty!

"After centuries of slavery, the Belgian, coming out of the tomb"...
Literally, this anthem speaks of a resurrection. A Lazarus
experience. A coming forth.

Also, a coming out of slavery, as Israel when it left Egypt
after 400 years of exile. The verses also speak of an untamed
people, following a King, in the name of righteousness and
freedom. Wow!

It refers to an old banner and honourable values, of courage,
of a reconquering of identity—*name!*—and flag.

Can you feel the Breath on those words?

Can you feel the trembling in the valley, the rattling of the bones?

Can you hear the coming of the Wind, from the four corners,
ready to realign the bones, join them bone to bone according
to divine order?

Call the prophetic intercessors, let them help, weep and groan in the Valley of Achor/*trouble*, let them water the plain where ground and bones are still dry. Let them feel the wound, the shock, the trauma, the offence, in order to release it. Let their heart of compassion travail on behalf of the land.[1] Stand in the gap, in the breach, on the fault line. Pray in this pivotal place where intercessors can strike the enemy at the heart.

Call the prophetic worshippers, let them sing in the valley of dry bones, till it is turned into a valley of hope.

Let them release the sound, the new sounds and rhythms, this "brand new and alien thing" that Isaiah was writing about.[2]

What would the mixing of Spanish rhythms, French words with Flemish dance be? Surely, the land would react to all that. But what it they could emerge in godly order and arrangement? Can you imagine the sound? Can you feel the walls of Jericho tremble? Can you see the Upper Room being shaken?

Son of man, what do you see? A bloodstained land, with very dry bones?

---

1 Most of the time, travailing prayer is a birthing prayer—it births something you've been carrying in your heart that God wants to deliver. But it can also be a deliverance prayer. For more of this, see the book by Jennifer LeClaire, *The Spiritual Warriors' Guide to Defeating Water Spirits*, Destiny Image Publishers, 2018.

2 See Isaiah 28:21

Can't you see words dancing before your eyes, wanting to be uttered, prophesied, released? Speak to the dry bones, call on the Breath.

Speak to Lazarus-Belgium: *Come forth!*

18. Turning the wound into a balm

When I shut up heaven and there is no rain, or command the locusts to devour the land, or send pestilence among My people, if My people who are called by My name will humble themselves, and pray and seek My face, and turn from their wicked ways, then I will hear from heaven, and will forgive their sin and heal their land.

2 Chronicles 7:12–14 NKJV

When you spread out your hands, I will hide My eyes from you; even though you make many prayers, I will not listen; your hands are full of blood.

Isaiah 1:15 ESV

Therefore I want the men in every place to pray, lifting up holy hands, without wrath and dissension.

1 Timothy 2:8 NASB

Belgium is known for many things abroad: chocolates, waffles, mussels and fries, beer, comic strips and surrealism...

But did you know it is also famous for bread? The bakery *Le Pain Quotidien* opened in 1990 in Brussels, then rapidly expanded through the years throughout Belgium (30 bakeries today) and then to 260 locations throughout the world! Read here how this charming bakery presents itself:[1]

> *"Join us at the table": Le Pain Quotidien means "the daily bread". And to us, that means everything. It's much more than mere sustenance; it's a way of life. As our loaves emerge from the ovens, warm and fragrant, friends gather around our communal tables to share in the time-honoured tradition of breaking bread...*

> *At Le Pain Quotidien, we believe that community is what nurtures, inspires and feeds the soul. Our first communal table in Brussels was built from wood salvaged from the floors of retired Belgian trains. Those simple planks became a tradition. Today, this same rough, reclaimed wood continues to bring a rustic comfort to our stores, and the communal tables have become our centrepiece.* [2]

Talk about storytelling! *Give us our daily bread. Come and join around the table.* [3]

---

1 See lepainquotidien.com/be/en/story.

2 The owner explains in the website that when he decided to open his bakery, he needed to decide on a name. He recalled a memory of his father exclaiming: "Moi, ce n'est pas mon pain quotidien!" literally translating to "It's not my daily bread!" He knew he needn't look any further for the words to hang above his bakery door. The website continues with these words, quite remarkably: "Welcome to *Le Pain Quotidien*, "the daily bread", where the past meets the present and the future is today!"

3 One week after the opening in October 1990, an article was published in the national newspaper *Le Soir* entitled: "Give us our daily bread." Following this article, the number of clients drastically increased and many restaurants began to buy their bread from them. From the book by Jean-Pierre Gabriel, *La table d'Alain Coumont: histoires et recettes*, Françoise Blouard, 2009.

Although the owner of *Le Pain Quotidien* is not known to be a professing Christian, this story of a Belgian bakery providing daily bread to the nation and nations sounds quite prophetic to me. If I open my spiritual ear, I begin to hear another storytelling, that could be very much in line with the identity and calling of Belgium:

> *Come to the table! Connect, cultivate relationships, bring what you have and it will be multiplied. Your loaves of bread. Your little fishes.*

> *Come as you are, do not pretend. It is family time. It is covenantal relationship. You can be yourself. You have to be yourself. As close proximity and deep sharing will soon ensure that any mantle of falsehood will be exposed, dis-mantled and fall apart.*

> *Come to the table and eat, drink, share.*
> *Soon bread and wine will be served and multiplied.*

> *Soon you will become the bread yourself, you will be broken and shared for the benefit of others, first in Jerusalem/Brussels, then to Samaria-Judea/ Flanders-Wallonia-German-speaking Belgium and further on, to the nations.*

By the way, aren't the nations already there, in your midst, in the streets of your capital city? Haven't they gathered for a long-ago-well-prepared Pentecost?

The day has not yet fully come, but is very much on its way.

A priesthood is getting prepared. A change of turban and priestly garment is happening, hidden from man's eyes. It happens in lockdown, in confinement, behind closed doors.

Forty days of preparation, of waiting, of lingering, of repenting, of speaking to the brother on the left and to the sister on the right and putting things right, where needed.

Now, that is the Biblical model, the heart of God, the condition for full release. Will you join in? Will you follow the blueprints? Will you build according to the model given?

The ones called to that table—which is also an Upper Room—you do not choose.

You have no say in this (s)election.

Only God chooses, and His criteria, are not yours.

Do not look to your personal preferences, do not despise what your eye does not yet recognise. After all, at first, Samuel misjudged who the *"anointed of the Lord"* was supposed to be.[4]

There is a great chance in this season that the Lord's choice will surprise you.

It is meant to shake and confront your comfort zones, your religious prejudices, your elitist *entre-soi*, in order to set you, and many others, free. It is meant to shake you out of your

---

4 See 1 Samuel 16:6 when, looking at Eliab, Samuel thinks that surely the Lord's anointed is before him.

sandals and put you again on the march, on the Way, moving, bearing fruit, all old branches cut off that were drying up your sap and making you barren.

That table—what it looks like, where it gathers, who takes the initiative—neither do you choose these things. Which form, how many seats—these are not yours to decide. The table is not even on this earth. Heavenly courts. Holy convocation.

The ones come who are called and have heard.

The shape of the table can change to accommodate the hosts—few or numerous. Yet this table is and will stay: a wheel inside a wheel. It is there to put you on the move.

Where the breach, the gap, the fault line has been, there comes the healing balm.

There the wound is transformed into a healing substance. Think of Géry of Cambrai; think of all the deep wounds of Belgium, of the trenches. Quality balm is on its way: oil is being poured over all kinds of wounds.

Also, the loaf of bread blessed and broken, into, through, over the midst. Where the crack was, there the light enters. The bread-loaf of Belgium is about to be blessed and broken and given to the nations. Was not this territory born as a buffer zone, prepared for all eternity to administer and to be administered for the benefit of others?

The sacrifice is being prepared, soon it will be on the altar.

If the loaf is about to be broken in two from its midst, will that happen along the old "limes wall" that once stood between the Roman and Germanic worlds and languages? Would Flanders be given as bread to the North and Wallonia to the South? Would Brussels be broken as bread for all the nations it hosts (hence the special taste, that the rest of the country does not always recognise as "His"?)

If so, the breaking would not mean disunity but sharing.

Unity of heart and purpose would still be there and make this "Kingdom of the Belgians" strong. The skingraft needed is a tabernacling[5] with the King of Kings, who gave His Body as a living sacrifice, for the benefit of all people, tribes and tongues.

So, maybe Flemish, Wallons and people from Brussels are finally allowed to be different, and understood in their differences: they do not have the same taste because they do not have to feed the same people...

Yet, in unity of calling and heart—feeding the nations—they can manage to stay One.

This unity not only *"makes us strong,"* as the Belgian motto says, but it is paramount in case of pestilence, locusts and all kinds of other adversities in order to heal the land.

---

5 A tabernacle was originally a tent of skin.

And here we come back to 2 Chronicles 7:14—*If My people who are called by My name will humble themselves, and pray and seek My face, and turn from their wicked ways, then I will hear from heaven, and will forgive their sin and heal their land.*

No proud look, no dishonour, no looking at others with a sense of superiority, no unforgiveness, no robbing others of their rights, no becoming strong at the expense of others.[6]

I will hear from heaven, and will forgive their sin and heal their land.

---

6 *Belgisch belang rather than Vlaams belang;* and healing of the wounds as it is often because it feels deprived that it needs to over-emphasise its own interests. Indeed, the Flemish nationalism also springs forth from wounds and injustice, and it remains so, because this has not been dealt with in-depth.

19. Releasing the governmental decrees

May the praise of God be in their mouths
and a double-edged sword in their hands,
to inflict vengeance on the nations
and punishment on the peoples,
to bind their kings with fetters,
their nobles with shackles of iron,
to carry out the sentence written against them—
this is the glory of all His faithful people.

Psalm 149:6–9 NIV

By Me kings reign, and rulers decree justice.

Proverbs 8:15 NKJV

Through the different chapters of this book, we have seen how throughout history, nations and kings, political and spiritual leaders, have gathered on this little piece of territory that today we know as Belgium.

We have seen them gather for the best and the worst reasons, for the best and worst results—shedding innocent blood, yet defeating the enemy; sacrificing one's life, yet fueling the fire of Reformation; turning, with the help of others, the battle at the gate during global conflict.

We have seen Brussels emerge as the governmental seat of authority (during Burgundian times as well as the empire of Charles V) and later become the capital city of the European Union, where administrative decrees are issued, and where legislation on different aspects of societal, political and economical life is passed.

We have begun to see the mandate of that city and country, the Levitical/priestly calling to make intercession for the nations, to stand in the gap and help unite, where the Leviathan-enemy would want to dismember, dis-joint.

There, where blood has been shed and decrees by man have been issued such as those of Philip II of Spain and the persecution of the Protestants, now the shedding of tears and the raising of holy hands and the issuing of spiritual decrees, can redeem.

Belgium, come forth! Have you not been called for such a time as this?

Belgium, make intercession for the European nations that gather on your territory and try to legislate!

Release holy governmental decrees!

Be priest, prophet and king: pray, declare and decree.

Have you not been born, raised, and soon to be healed, for such a time as this?

Where Haman has the decree written and the gallows built to execute the chosen people, governmental cities, as "Esther-cities", must seize their spiritual weapons of prayer, fasting and decreeing to cancel and nullify the unrighteous acts and proclamations. Levites must gather, join, re-member.

Books should be reopened as kings and civil servants are kept awake by a Spirit trying to remind them of something.

A calling, a mandate, a destiny.
A time and season. A *kairos* time.
A place and strategic location, at the heart.

Remind them of words spoken: *strike at the heart!*
–   Of images seen: Sint-Michaël defeating the dragon.
–   Of legends heard: Sint Géry building a church in the name of Michaël—and defeating another dragon.
–   Of books written: King Albert's book, *A Tribute to The Belgian King and People*, the courage and valour of brave little Belgium.
–   Of books written in heaven, blueprints yet to be revealed, yet already foreshadowed.

A story of joining, of sharing bread rather than shedding blood, of tables prepared, of leaders gathering, making plans, re-reading maps, remembering chapters of dishonour in history and repenting, asking forgiveness to one another, wailing at the wall together, making reparations where possible.

Then, strong, as one, coming forth, coming out, making preparations on behalf of others, writing and uttering decrees, raising holy hands.

Could that be the calling/destiny of Belgium? With the buffer zone and "blood sacrifice" as a counterfeit? Could that be the nature of a central Levitical tribe—as opposed to a centralised Leviathan empire?

Think of what could happen when honour is restored to the priesthood, when clean hands can rise again in intercession. Remember again 2 Chronicles 7:13–17. Remember that the words were given after the dedication of the Temple—the temple of Solomon:

> *When I shut up the heavens so that there is no rain, or command locusts to devour the land or send a plague among my people, if my people, who are called by My name, will humble themselves and pray and seek My face and turn from their wicked ways, then I will hear from heaven, and I will forgive their sin and will heal their land. Now My eyes will be open and My ears attentive to the prayers offered in this place. I have chosen and consecrated this temple so that My Name may be there forever. My eyes and My heart will always be there.*

Jesus is the right and righteous cornerstone for the Levitical priesthood and tribe. He is also the rejected cornerstone. And in His place have come counterfeits: other cornerstones present in the institutions, temples and crafts of the land.

There is a saying about Belgian architecture—the so-called "skieven architek",[1] which speaks of a way of building that is not right but "askew". Does this reveal the existence of a faulty foundation?

If so, let us bring back the true cornerstone with shouts of *Grace! Grace!*

And let us remember, as Belgium has no king, that there is room on this territory for a King of Kings!

Selah.
Pause.
Quietly consider.
And rejoice.

---

1 "Schieven Architek" was the name given to Joseph Poelaert, the architect of the largest Justice Palace in the world (also qualified as mammoth or pharaonic). In the Brussels dialect, *schieven* means "askew". See, for instance, lecho.be/dossier/130ans/le-palais-polemique-du-skieven-architek/9062518.html.

Appendix 1

Birth trauma
Jean-Antoine

The way Belgium was born may have been somewhat traumatic. This book evokes this aspect. In short, the creation of the country emanates from the will of neighbouring great powers to create a buffer zone between their empires, in order to protect their interests. The will of the indigenous peoples was of little importance. We can therefore reasonably speak of a traumatic birth, having resulted in the alliance of peoples with quite different backgrounds and cultures.

"Nations are like human beings," said a pastor during intercessory training. This meant that the reactional processes and the spiritual consequences that one can find in a human being, after a traumatic event, can be found in a similar way at the level of nations in the face of traumas in their history.

What happens when a person is born can have real consequences throughout their life. This can influence their very relationship to life and the way it will develop.

The same goes for the birth of a country. If it is experienced in a traumatic way by the peoples who constitute it, the inhabitants are at great risk of developing post-traumatic symptoms, which will manifest themselves both psychically and spiritually. Deleterious and pernicious patterns of life can become a permanent part of the functioning of the citizens who experienced this birth, as well as their descendants. The very institutions of the country could also be strongly imbued with it.

From a spiritual point of view, spirits will be able to take advantage of this birth trauma, more specifically of its consequences: the suffering and the sin which will result from it, to make a lasting alliance with the nation, in an insidious way. And, as long as these alliances, even hidden ones, are not exposed and broken, they will influence the life of the country and its inhabitants.

Take this passage from Ezekiel in the Bible that talks about a traumatic birth:

> *And as for your birth, on the day you were born your cord was not cut, nor were you washed with water to cleanse you, nor rubbed with salt, nor wrapped in swaddling cloths. No eye pitied you, to do any of these things to you out of compassion for you, but you were cast out on the open field, for you were abhorred, on the day that you were born. And when I passed by you and saw you wallowing in your blood, I said to you in your blood, 'Live!' I said to you in your blood, 'Live!' I made you flourish like a plant of the field. And you grew up and became tall and arrived at full adornment. Your breasts were formed, and your hair had grown; yet you were naked and bare.*

> Ezekiel 16:4–7 ESV

In context, this is the symbolic account of the birth of Jerusalem. But this story is not unlike that of the birth of Belgium.

We can note the lack of care given to this child. From a physical point of view, it has not been washed, the umbilical cord has not been cut, nor has proper care been taken of it. It has not been rubbed with salt, supposedly to strengthen it and give it vigor. It has not been changed or dressed. It therefore remains as it is: born certainly, but abandoned without help or vital care.

Emotionally, this child received neither love nor even compassion for his condition. Worse, he caused a feeling of horror among those who gave birth to him and he experienced complete rejection: left alone in the middle of a field, exposed to certain death.

While the birth process may have gone relatively well, the perinatal events were, to say the least, traumatic for this child. And the consequences of all this are going to be catastrophic.

The fact, therefore, that this is the symbolic account of the birth of Jerusalem, a city and a people, is central to our understanding of things. This allows us to realise that "it is with nations as with human beings." The city of Jerusalem and its people have been personified and their history reduced to that of a young child and her difficult birth.

We see, if we look at the rest of chapter 16 of Ezekiel, that this "young-girl-people" will develop deadly attitudes and behaviour. She will develop behaviour that will be abominable in the eyes of the Lord. Despite the care that He will lavish on her so that she can still grow and develop, she will put her confidence in herself, in her own beauty. She will begin to be adulterous and to prostitute herself to lovers among neighboring peoples and among foreign gods.

She will be weak of heart (v. 30), unstable in her emotions and feelings, with a poor self-image; to the point of paying her lovers to take advantage of her as a prostitute. The latter will, therefore, develop contempt and hatred towards her. They will go so far as to humiliate her and try to destroy her.

This "young-girl-people" will break the holy covenant which she had made with her Creator, depriving herself of the intimacy of the relationship with the One who nevertheless kept and nurtured her. In her pride and rebellion, by breaking this covenant with the Lord and making covenants with others, she will sink into self-destructive and deadly attitudes, which will slowly destroy her and deeply hurt the One who had helped her.

The same goes for nations that experience traumatic births or traumatic perinatal conditions. There is a good chance that similar behavioural and emotional consequences will develop in them. It is very likely that they will enter into questionable covenants and turn away from the true source of life which is the Lord, the God of Abraham, Isaac and Jacob.

The consequences of traumatic births

Traumatic births or traumatic perinatal events can lead to various consequences that we will name, without having the space to go into all the details that this problem deserves.

However, to sum up, such births can cause a reversal of life reflexes and death reflexes, as well as what we might call a "void wound" (*blessure de néant*, in French).

Regarding the inversion of life reflexes into death reflexes, we can say that when a child is born, it is logical that he goes towards life. The whole process of birth, which passes through the vagina through the mother's contractions, is designed to give the child the impetus to come to life with vigour. He acquires a fighting force and reflexes which push him towards life.

But if, unfortunately, this passage goes badly or is upset, the reflexes of life risk turning into a reflex of death. For example, if the baby has the umbilical cord wrapped around his neck during the passage, he will strangle and feel as if he is dying just when he is supposed to feel himself fully entering into life. He will then associate life with death and his patterns, like his reflexes, will therefore develop in a *deadly* sense, in the strict sense of the word: *towards death*. For him, going towards life will be the same as going towards death. He then risks confusing the impulses of life with the impulses of death. If these consequences are not addressed in prayer, there is a risk that the child, and later the adult, will not be able to discern the difference between life and death, nor between the covenant of life and covenants of death. It is then that one or more spirits of death can take hold, as well as a death mindset.

There are real similarities with what Ezekiel reports (chapter 16) concerning the behaviour of Jerusalem, the deadly covenants it made, as well as its denial of the covenant of life with the Creator.

The wound of nothingness

My friend Beatriz Gaillet teaches the concept of the wound of 'nothingness'. This is a type of injury that can appear during trauma, including traumatic birth or perinatal abandonment.

In the perinatal context, this wound of nothingness often occurs when a feeling of "descent into death" occurs—when, in these moments, one should be moving towards life.

This feeling of death and annihilation—where the name "nothingness wound" comes from—stems from a feeling of imminent risk of death, whether through direct risk of dying or from lack of care. Indeed, an infant, if he does not receive the care his state of dependence requires, nor the affection he needs, will feel in real danger of death. He then risks developing this wound of nothingness and opening himself up to the influence of death where, precisely, there should have been life.

Live in your blood

The good news of Ezekiel 16 is that the Lord is filled with love and compassion. When He passes by a person or a nation that is going through this birth trauma, He says to them: *"Live! Live in your blood."* (Ezekiel 16:6)

The Lord has for each person and for each nation, *"plans for well-being, and not for calamity, in order to give you a future and a hope."* (Jeremiah 29:11 ISV) Jesus came so that we could have "life in abundance" and even in excess. (See John 10:10)

Our God is El Shaddai. Which, in Hebrew, means *He is the one who can give life to that which no longer had life.* It also means that He is a *nurturer* and that He will be able to *nourish* the person or the nation until it is able to *develop and flourish.*

His love and concern will continue throughout our lives. Even if after restoration we may not yet remain fully faithful to Him, He will continue to remain faithful and call us to leave our evil ways, to repent, and to come back to Him. This is the attitude He takes throughout Ezekiel 16 towards Jerusalem. This is the attitude He also takes towards us and towards our nations.

Our Lord Jesus claims the nations as His inheritance (Psalm 2:7–9), even those who have experienced birth trauma and have entered into deadly and demonic alliances.

Shall we work with Him in their redemption, their deliverance, their healing and their restoration?

El Shaddai says: *"Live in your blood."*

Appendix 2

Poem

John Roedel

(Proposed here as a lullaby for Belgium; reproduced with John's permission.)

The journey from
being wounded
to being healed
will take exactly
as long as it needs to
I know you want
to rush to get
your scar as
soon as you can
but my love,
recovery isn't mean to be a race
it's often a slow walk
down a five-mile
curvy country road
take your time
coming back
to yourself
let your repairs
happen carefully

mend your heart
like it is a cathedral
that is being
gently restored
one carefully laid
brick
mosaic tile
and shard of stained glass
at a time
my love,
your scars will come to you in time
and someday they will teach you
but in the meantime,
nurse your wound like a
newborn
slowly
thoughtfully
and with the softest of thoughts
my love,
the sound of your heart
makes as it heals
is my most favourite psalm
don't rush through the verses
of your sacred recuperation
let your lyrics echo
let them linger
let them dawdle
let them in hang in the air
like fireflies
until they surround you
and help you stand on
your feet again

your comeback
starts now
not with a footrace
on hard pavement
but rather, your return
to yourself will begin
with a meandering walk
down a stretching dirt path
under a cotton candy sky
my love, oh my love,
don't set your watch
to your healing
don't give it
a deadline
instead
give it all the time it needs
to remind you
how incredibly
beautiful you
look
when you heal

John Roedel
Poet, writer, storyteller
Author of *Hey God. Hey John*
www.johnroedel.com

Afterword

Ignace Demaerel

Even when other nations designed Belgium as a buffer zone, God was in the process and He knew the future already: He allowed it with a purpose! And He can make all things, also this one, work for good.

I strongly believe that if we, Belgians, can accept this mandate of a buffer/peace zone, not as externally forced on us, but as a way of joyfully serving the other nations (not being a ruling country but serving with joy), this would be great. Not wanting "to be as big as the others" (jealousy), but being humble (which makes us great in God's eyes).

We can indeed complain about the many divisions or problems in our nation but we should also be aware that many other nations in the world have much of this (cultures and languages, and wars, bloodshed, birth trauma…)

May God grant us the grace to see the positive side of it and rejoice in diversity.

My main question about repentance/healing for Belgium's past is:

(1) who has to do it? (who has the authority, is in the right position…?) *and*

(2) when is it finished? when do we know that the process is completed and the trauma healed?

Food for (further) thought...

Acknowledgments

To my parents and siblings, for the price that was paid, "bridging the gap" between two languages, cultures, religions and heritages.

To Anne Griffith, prophet to the nations, "mother in Israël", faithful lover of Belgium.

To Anne Hamilton, author and publisher, who helps the Body of Christ worldwide with strategies for the thresholds and other precious revelations.

To Ignace Demaerel, pastor, author, leader of Pray4Belgium, for his dedication to our land, and for having reread the first draft of this book and help improve some parts.

To Jean-Antoine, author and friend, for having interceded and wept often with me for our land, and for his valuable contribution about the consequences of traumatic birth.

To Moyra Sims, who has helped improve the English of a non-native speaker/ writer.

To John Roedel, wonderful poet, for writing authentic words of life that bring comfort to the heart and for allowing me to reproduce his incredible text about *The journey from being wounded to being healed* (John, if you read this: you are one of my favourite contemporary writers, your pen is a blessing to the Body of Christ and beyond!)

To Paul Verheul for his inspired painting, variation on the flag of Belgium, reproduced on the cover of this book.

To all the ones who, through the years have faithfully plowed the soil of this land with prayer: Ignace and Miet, Luc and Agnès, Rik and Sabine, Yves and Liliane, Jean-Claude and Berry... and many others, both from Belgium and abroad.

To God, for having led and let me write about Belgium, for His unfailing love and perfect guidance (Last mentioned, but surely not Least).

www.facebook.com/deborah.dekker.3